21 HACKS to ROCK *your* LIFE

STOP PROCRASTINATING, DO THAT THING AND LIVE A LIFE ON-PURPOSE!

CAT COLUCCIO

First published 2019 by Cat Coluccio

Produced by Indie Experts P/L, Australasia
indieexperts.com.au

Copyright © Cat Coluccio 2019

The moral right of the author to be identified as the author of this work has been asserted.

All rights reserved. Except as permitted under the *Australian Copyright Act 1968*, no part of this publication may be reproduced, stored in a retrieval system, or transmitted in any form or by any means, electronic, mechanical, photocopying, recording or otherwise, without prior written permission from the publisher. All enquiries should be made to the author.

Cover design by Maria Biaggini @ Indie Experts
Edited by Libby Turner
Internal design by Indie Experts
Typeset in 11.5/15.5 pt Minion Pro by Post Pre-press Group, Brisbane

ISBN 978-0-6487029-0-0 (paperback)
ISBN 978-0-6487029-2-4 (epub)
ISBN 978-0-6487029-1-7 (kindle)

Disclaimer:
The material in this book is provided for information purposes only. The experiences discussed in this book may not necessarily be the same as the reader's experience. The reader should consult with his or her personal legal, financial and other advisors before utilising the information contained in this book. The author and the publisher assume no responsibility for any damages or losses incurred during or as a result of following this information.

For Darlene.
Known as the queen of systems and order to all who knew her. The ultimate organiser of pantries, kitchens, offices and paperwork. Lover of Sauvignon Blanc, Prosecco, books, music, theology and her family. My precious friend for over 20 years.
I miss you.

CONTENTS

Foreword	vii
Introduction	xi

SECTION 1: MIND HACKS — 1
Hack #1	Visualization	3
Hack #2	Do Not Multitask!	12
Hack #3	Breathe!	15

SECTION 2: PHYSICAL ENVIRONMENT HACKS — 21
Hack #4	Clear the Clutter!	23
Hack #5	Ditch the Open-Space Office	27
Hack #6	Block the Noise!	31

SECTION 3: HEALTH AND WELLBEING HACKS — 35
Hack #7	Ditch the Snooze Button!	37
Hack #8	Move that Body!	42
Hack #9	Nourish Yourself!	47
Hack #10	Drink that Water!	52

SECTION 4: TIME HACKS   55
    Hack #11 Clear the Forest so You Can See the Trees 57
    Hack #12 Map Your Wheel of Life 62
    Hack #13 Knock Off the Hard Stuff First! 68
    Hack #14 Use a Timer! 74

SECTION 5: ATTITUDE HACKS   79
    Hack #15 Find Your Pedestal 81
    Hack #16 Establish Your Boundaries 86
    Hack #17 Choose Your Mood 91

SECTION 6: ACCELERATION HACKS   97
    Hack #18 Implement Systems 99
    Hack #19 Create Your Dream Team 108

SECTION 7: ACTION HACKS   115
    Hack #20 Intentional Action 117
    Hack #21 Start Today! 123

A Final Word From Cat 129
Acknowledgements 133
About Cat Coluccio 137
Want More Cat? 139
Endnotes 141
References 145

FOREWORD

"Not another time-management book," I hear you groan!

Relax – this is not another dry how-to-schedule-your-life tome that you will lose interest in after the first chapter then use it to prop your door open. Trust me.

My years of personal experience and research have helped me discover numerous practical hacks that have made a huge difference in my life, and which I know will make a difference in yours too. These hacks have the potential to help you build mindset, wellness and time-management strategies, and to ultimately create the action steps to live a fulfilled and on-purpose life. In short, they will help you ROCK your life – and this makes me super happy as helping people rock their lives by living "ON-purpose" is my *raison d'être*. What's even better is that the hacks can generally be applied right away, meaning you don't have to wait until next Monday, or until you have the right equipment, location, income or *whatever* to get started!

It doesn't matter if the goal you are wanting to achieve is in your workplace or in your domestic world, as these 21 hacks will work for both. Just imagine, by committing to learning and applying one new hack each day, you could find your life transformed in just 21 days! Instead of feeling like you struggle to maintain your wellbeing, are always scrambling for time, are busy yet producing little or are weighed down by the realisation that you are not fully achieving your life's purpose – you now have in your hand a plan to help you turn your life around.

Just pause a minute, shut your eyes and picture yourself *doing* that thing that you really want to achieve and ROCKING your life:

Being confident and fulfilled in your work.

Being productive and on-task in your daily routine.

Having a healthy, strong body and a positive, disciplined mind.

Actually *achieving* that thing that you feel you are called to do.

Living a life that is ON-purpose, where your choices and decisions are in alignment with what you feel that you were truly made for.

Doesn't this mental image make you feel great? Why would you ever again settle for anything less?

Let today be the first day of your journey to living your life on purpose. If there is one thing that I have learned over the years, it is that life is short and precious – so it is time to stop wasting it, time to *do that thing* that your heart is calling you to do and time to ROCK your life!

Cat

PS: Want some quick tips to help you get stuff done? Go to https://bit.ly/3Otips and get a FREE checklist: ***30 Tips to Help you ROCK your Productivity!***

INTRODUCTION

Who feels like their brain is in a constant state of overload these days? The average person is already overwhelmed before they even leave the house. Laundry, food preparation, house and yard upkeep, child rearing, pet care, finances, insurances, vehicle maintenance, family occasions and holiday planning just to name a few. I have only scratched the surface of all the tasks that need to be done.

On leaving the house, Mr or Ms Average head to their workplace where they are bombarded with the weight of further responsibilities and activities, including emails, phone calls, client demands, content creation, social media, marketing, budgeting, meetings, presentations, conferences and seminars, and so on.

All the while, their phones ping relentlessly with a stream of notifications: news, stocks, weather, Facebook, Instagram, Snapchat, WhatsApp, LinkedIn, text and call alerts.

Is it any wonder that we are more stressed and burned out than ever, despite having access to more time-saving tools and programs than any previous generation?

Meet Mike. Mike is a bit of a hipster in his mid- to late-30s. He can be identified by his funky little beard, plaid retro shirt and flat cap. He likes to ride his bike as much as possible and can often be heard pontificating the lack of urban greenspaces over a flat white to his equally hip colleagues in their open plan office. Underneath his cool exterior however, is a man running himself ragged. He is doing everything he can to try to be an engaged husband, father and a provider for his young family all the while staying competitive in his workplace so that he can find advancement and fulfilment in his career. He does all of this while trying to keep physically healthy. He has no time for illness, especially considering the latest new up-and-coming, tech-savvy and job-hungry graduates interning at his workplace.

The minute Mike gets home of an evening, a screaming toddler is generally thrust into his arms as his equally frazzled wife tries to help their five-year-old with his spelling. Following the dinner/clean-up/ kids to bed frenzy, Mike grabs a beer, crashes in front of Netflix in a state of exhaustion and checks his phone for more notifications and emails to respond to before he starts to nod off. Later, in bed, he struggles with broken sleep as thoughts of tomorrow's meetings play in his mind.

Then there is Mike's wife, Alice. Alice is also exhausted trying to sustain a marriage and a career, with the added bonus that once she gets in the door of an evening, she faces the lion's share of the housework, homework supervision, planning of the family schedule, laundry and tomorrow's lunch preparation. Not to mention tonight's dinner, whatever the heck *that* is going to be …

The minute the kids are in bed, she is sculling a glass or two of wine while throwing yet another load of washing on before she too settles down to check her emails and social media notifications. Her husband is already starting to snore on the couch by the time she sits down, and she shuffles him off to bed. She has minimal sleep due to her brain going over tomorrow's to-do lists for the family, and also fretting over the incomplete report that her boss is expecting on his desk in the morning.

Mike and Alice are worn-out, stressed and not happy.

They are busy but, like the proverbial hamster on the wheel, they are not really productive, merely getting the basics done in order to survive.

There is food on the table and a roof over their heads, but at the same time, their wellness and satisfaction with life are below average. They feel overwhelmed with tasks but don't feel like they have time to do the things that they actually *want* to do.

This is a discontent that comes with feeling that they are not really living "on purpose" and in short, they are not *rocking* their lives.

Does any of this sound familiar? I bet it does.

The exciting thing is that things can change for the better and you don't need to continue feeling like you are starring in your own version of the movie *Groundhog Day*. There are numerous actions you can take that will help you simplify and streamline your days, creating that desired commodity that you think is out of reach … time.

Time to reconnect with your partner and family.

Time to practise self-care and wellness.

Time to do the things that bring you joy, be that to go fishing, write a book or volunteer.

Sound good?

These 21 hacks to help you ROCK your life are by no means a finite list of ideas to help you work towards your goals and live "on-purpose." They do however provide a starting point which, if you take action, will help you to establish patterns of behavior which will help create the foundations of life changing habits.

I challenge you now to commit to not just reading these hacks, but to really consider them. To take the time to think through the Action Tasks that accompany each hack and, most importantly, actually *take* massive, imperfect, messy action for each one.

Are you ready to hack your way to creating a life that rocks?

Read on!

"You'll never change your life until you change something you do daily. The secret of your success is found in your daily routine."

JOHN. C. MAXWELL

SECTION 1

MIND HACKS

"You have power over your mind – not outside events. Realize this, and you will find strength."

~ MARCUS AURELIUS

HACK #1
Visualization

"I believe that visualization is one of the most powerful means of achieving personal goals."
~ HARVEY MACKAY

There is increasing evidence supporting the link between visualization and reaching for a goal. When conducted intentionally, visualization can be a powerful tool that not only redirects neural pathways or patterns of thinking, but can affect physical performance as well. If you can visualize clearly the thing you want to achieve, you have a far greater chance of actually achieving it.

A study was conducted in recent years on the "Effect of a psychological skills training program on swimming performance and positive psychological development,"[1] where 36 national-level swimmers were taken through a 45 min PST (psychological skills training) session every week. As well as visualization, the PST training also covered the setting of goals, relaxation and concentration techniques and how to stop thoughts.

The results were definitive: without any extra physical training designed to focus on particular strokes and distances, the swimmers as a group exhibited significant improvements in three differing swimming strokes. As well, there were other improvements demonstrated in other events and the group's overall psychological profiles also were positively impacted as a result of the PST program. When you consider that this was achieved through the addition of psychological skills training to their regular physical training, which particularly emphasized visualization, the results of this study are exciting! Ask yourself this question: "what could I *really* achieve if I applied the same technique to skills that I am trying to master?"

The positive physical effects of visualization are to be applauded, but let's take it a little further and ask ourselves what would be the impact of having a positive attitude and outlook in general? Without a positive attitude, we risk giving up on our dreams and goals as soon as our mood changes. Depending how reactionary we are, our moods have the ability to change numerous times a day. If we don't have the ability to hold to an overarching positive "super mood" that links us to our goal, we run the very real risk of our varying emotions directly affecting our every action.

Interestingly, there is a study titled "Manipulating optimism: Can imagining a best possible self be used to increase positive future expectancies?"[2] that looked to test if students who wrote about and visualized becoming their future best selves developed a more robust, positive outlook for the future. Those students who did visualize what they wanted to become ended up holding far higher and more positive expectations for the future. What was even more crucial though, was that they managed to develop and maintain an overarching positive attitude towards their goal – an attitude that was not swayed by passing emotions. Imagine going through the usual rollercoaster emotions of life but not having your inner expectations and dreams for a better future squashed in the process? How much more resilient could you become in bouncing back into gear and pressing towards your goal after facing a setback?

Now, while I am all about the action we are taking in this first hack of visualization, it is important to understand the science behind the action so that you can quiet that little voice in your head that tries to tell you that you are being silly when you take the time to visualize where you want to be. I'm sure that even after reading about these studies, while there is part of you that really wants to give it a go, there is another that is is scoffing at the notion.

Let's take a brief look at the brain. Your brain is bombarded daily with millions of pieces of information. Thankfully, we operate on default mode 40–49% of the time, otherwise our brain would melt down with the amount of decisions it would have to deal with.

Can you imagine ever getting anything done if you had to debate the pros and cons of *if* you should clean your teeth, *why* you should clean your teeth, *which* toothbrush you should use, *why* is that one the best choice, *which* toothpaste to apply, etc. *every single day*?

Default mode enables us to continue functioning while leaving mental space to deal with unique or more pressing decisions. However, it does have its down side.

We have an inbuilt "filter" known as the Reticular Activating System (RAS) which is a group of nerves at the brain stem. The primary purpose of the RAS is to filter the massive amounts of information that we encounter every minute and to only let the important stuff through. This can lead to filtering only information that supports our point of view and can contribute to the phenomena of confirmation bias. Think of when you decided to purchase a new model of car. Not only do they suddenly seem to appear everywhere, but you seem to be discovering new information daily that supports your decision to choose that make and model. Articles seem to appear singing that model's praises and you suddenly notice billboards featuring that car. Your RAS is filtering information now to support your decision to purchase.

Now, imagine if your RAS is set to support default thinking that you are *not* able to transform your life? Imagine if you were finding confirming information everywhere that showed you that you were correct in thinking yourself stuck and unable to do that thing you really want to do? Imagine if the only voices you heard out of all of the people you speak to were the negative ones telling you that you could never change? Imagine if your own inner voice was constantly informing you that you are not able to, not worthy of and will *never* have a life that rocks?

Your filter is doing its job of sifting out everything except the information that confirms your innermost thoughts and beliefs, which is why if you are to truly start DOING that thing and ROCKING your life, it is time to reprogram your Reticular Activating System. This will set you up for a transformational experience – you will be set up to win! You won't be fighting against yourself or wondering why you can never get a breakthrough like all of the other times where you have tried but failed. This time will be very different.

Excited?

You should be and I am excited for you. I have witnessed many clients make various transformations over the years, yet I've also been disheartened when so many others could not sustain the transformation that they said they desperately wanted. I've spent hours beating myself up and wondering what was wrong with me as a coach and often questioned whether the client really *wanted* to change.

Learning about the power of changing our thinking from the very core, beginning with changing our filter, has been life-changing for myself personally and in turn, for my clients. Now we know how to set ourselves up for a real and lasting transformation – and that is powerful!

But back to visualization. The starting point in changing the filter in our brain, and the very first practical hack that you are going to apply. It's possibly the *most* important hack too, so make sure that you don't skip over it, but take the time to learn the steps properly, then grab a pen and mark in your diary when you are going to repeat it.

ACTION TASKS:

- Find a room where you will not be interrupted by people, pets or technology.
- Leave your cellphone in another room and sit yourself down somewhere comfortable.
- It's important now to close your eyes. Try to see yourself as having made the transformation you want to make. You might see yourself healthy and fit as you complete a triathlon. You might see yourself at your graduation ceremony with that degree you decided to study for. You might see yourself confidently walking out of your boss's office with a promotion. You create the picture that represents YOUR personal transformation.
- Now, make sure that you add color to the picture. Add noise, scents and movement. Include every sense and make that picture as real as possible.
- Hold that picture in your mind for a few minutes. Ask yourself "What am I feeling in this picture?" Allow yourself to really FEEL the emotion of having made that transformation. This is critical, as we also want to stimulate the limbic system in your brain which affects emotions and memories. Researchers have discovered that the brain does not distinguish reality from imagination, so the more emotion and details applied to the image, the more that it will be recognized by the brain as fact. I often have clients "ground" this emotion even more powerfully by smelling an essential oil, usually the gorgeous

Wild Orange, known as the "oil of abundance." Smell is the primary sense associated with the limbic system and putting a connection between that scent and the positive feelings of achieving your transformation will provide a powerful connection.
- As well as asking yourself how you are feeling in your visualization, I want you to ask sensory questions. What are you wearing? Where are you located? What noises can you hear? Can you feel anything? (e.g. the wind on your face, waves at your feet).
- Create a mental image that is so strong and so well-rounded that it completely feels like you are in that moment. Hold it as long as possible, then repeat this action at least twice a day for the next 30 days.

It will be life changing, I can guarantee you.

You will be amazed at how you start to find yourself noticing more and more information that confirms the image that you see of yourself. You'll start to feel excitement bubbling up in you as your default mode no longer leans to the negative but instead brings hope, joy and expectation.

I suspect that your initial reaction is "who has time to sit around like that?" so let's reframe that thinking right away with some strong affirming statements:

> "I have ALL the time I need to complete my visualization exercise twice a day."

"I WANT to complete my visualization exercise twice a day."

"I'm EXCITED to complete my visualization exercise twice a day."

Feeling the emotions of these statements and saying them out loud is also reprogramming your RAS so that you will not be struggling to do your exercise, but will *want* to do it.

Now put this book down, find that quiet space and do it!

HACK #2
Do Not Multitask!

There are many studies that show the decline in efficiency of the brain and behavior of a person engaged in multitasking. In the past, this may have meant reading the newspaper while eating your lunch, however multitasking has become such a normalized behavior these days that we find ourselves doing it virtually every minute. Who else has eaten dinner while watching Netflix, simultaneously scrolling Facebook and responding to instant messages and texts on your phone?

Who can't even visit the bathroom without checking the latest posts on Instagram? (Guilty as charged with this one!)

We feel more productive when multitasking but the reality is that if we stand back and examine dispassionately what we are *actually* achieving, the result is generally very little. We are caught up responding and reacting to other people's wants and needs and can find that an entire day slips past where we have not done the thing that would actually move us towards the success or state that we desire.

A study entitled "Higher Media Multi-Tasking Activity Is Associated with Smaller Gray-Matter Density in the Anterior Cingulate Cortex" confirms what many productivity specialists have long thought – that multi-tasking – particularly of media sources – negatively affects cognitive response and also impacts relational interactions.[3] In reality though, anyone who is a parent doesn't need a study to tell them that Johnny's homework is not going to be too coherent if he has been simultaneously watching TV, texting and scrolling social media while trying to write his essay!

By choosing to focus on one task fully at a time, you will find that your productivity is greater and the number of errors you make diminished. Your brain has the chance to be fully engaged and is allowed to function far more optimally than if you force it to divide its attention between rapidly changing distractions. You also eliminate the wasted minutes that add up throughout a day when you force your brain to change gears and jump from task to task. Every time that you divert from that writing project to check your mail, then while responding to that, check to your calendar and answer a pop up message – you are losing time as your brain has to scramble to process this new data. Want to find more time in the day? Stick to the one task at hand and shut down those other distractions!

Eliminating the lure of multitasking, is setting yourself up to find the time and space you desire to truly focus on to *achieve* that thing that you haven't been able to get done and ROCK your on-purpose life!

ACTION TASKS:

- To limit your time on social media, which is probably the main distraction to staying on task these days, the simplest action you can take is to turn on the airplane mode of your phone or tablet whenever you sit down to focus on a task. Even as I am writing this book, my electronics are all in airplane mode, and the phone is even face down and out of reach so that I don't habitually pick it up to check. I know of many authors and entrepreneurs who actually leave their phones in another room until they have finished a priority task that requires all of their focus. There are also numerous apps and programs you can download to limit your access.
- Decide today whenever you sit down to work on a particular task, whether it be at your workplace or while helping your children with their homework, that you will choose to remove your electronic devices and purposely determine to focus on the *one* thing in front of you.

HACK #3
Breathe!

As mentioned earlier, our brains like to work in "default" mode. This is great in that it saves us the stress of having to make literally thousands of decisions every day. However, our default is generally set to survival mode, meaning we are primed to be looking for any indication of danger in order to alert the body to take flight, to freeze or to fight. This means – and I'm sorry to break this to you – that we are never truly free of negative pressure. Living with a certain level of stress is our natural state.

A problem arises when our already danger-hunting "spider senses" become too sensitive. The feelings of stress can start to overwhelm us, causing physiological reactions like shallow breathing, chest pain, insomnia, muscle tension and anxiety along with behavioral reactions such as procrastination and lack of focus. We don't do the things we *should* be doing to create a rocking life … and then we dwell on the fact that we aren't doing what we should be doing! We distract ourselves with technology or food and alcohol, then beat ourselves up so that we feel even more stressed and overwhelmed. Then our vicious cycle continues, round and around we go …

The buzz word of the moment is "mindfulness" and it is a key factor in breaking this cycle of our primate survival brain spiralling out of control. The word may immediately make you think of yoga and woo-woo chanting but mindfulness is really nothing more than the practice of harnessing the frantic, stressed mind, bringing it into the present moment and allowing it to calm down.

The creator of the modern mindfulness movement is scientist Jon Kabat-Zinn, who came up with the strategy of the S.T.O.P technique, an easily learned technique which can be used whenever we feel that our stress response is gaining momentum.[4] It causes us to pause, get perspective and then respond to the task in front of us in a considered manner as opposed to a reactive state. There have been lots of variations of this technique created as people seek ways to pause and reduce the feeling of overwhelm in their day, resulting in numerous mindfulness and breathing-focused apps now available. Even my watch reminds me to pause and breathe when it is not bugging me to stand and move!

My own background as a professional musician, in particular, a woodwind player, means that learning to breathe properly was critical if I wanted to play beyond a few notes without passing out. In the early days of learning the saxophone, my teacher used to perform an exercise to help me feel what it was like to breathe properly. He would make me lay down and place a book on my stomach which would rise as I took in a deep breath. Simultaneously, my stomach would expand as my diaphragm moved down so that my lungs could fill to capacity. Had he said "take a deep breath" while I was standing – I would have done the same thing that I have watched literally hundreds of students do over the years that I conducted bands and worked with choirs: I would have sucked in air while raising my shoulders to my ears. The result? The diagram would have been sucked upwards, and I would only have filled the upper part of my lungs with air.

When studying for my degree at the Conservatorium in Sydney, an opera teacher who would demand that we "open the intercostals!" as she squeezed our ribs hard, would make us wear firm bands wrapped around our rib cages under our clothing which we were to push out against all through the day. The intercostal muscles are located between the ribs and expand and shrink the chest cavity making them critical to the mechanics of breathing. In her own creative way, this teacher was giving us something tangible to push against so that we could learn the sensation of expansion that we needed to train our muscles to do automatically. Without this training, we would not be able to breathe effectively enough to power our voices for performance.

Even if you don't want to blow an instrument or sing on stage, your breathing has a direct physical and a psychological impact on your mental and physical wellbeing and with practise, is something that you can learn to affect you positively. If you pause in the midst of overwhelm, pressure and busyness to take note of how you are breathing, you might be surprised to discover that you are just like those choir members that I worked with: your shoulders are tense, your breathing is shallow and you feel agitated and jittery. Breathing like this causes stress hormones to be heightened even further than where they are already at and you might even be unconsciously hyperventilating, creating a vicious cycle of feeling even more stressed and overwhelmed as you physically add to the overwhelming mental load you are already carrying.

It's time to break the cycle of stress and overwhelm and take the time to learn how to breathe your way back into the present moment, so that you can still your mind, calm your body and restore your focus on achieving that thing that you are wanting to do.

ACTION TASKS:

- Find yourself a large book, lay down on your back and place it on your stomach. Take your time to breathe deeply and shallowly, noting the different sensation between your lungs being half empty and filled to capacity.
- Now stand in front of a mirror and continue to practise breathing deeply. Watch to see if you can take a deep breath without raising your shoulders. Turn side on and try to expand your stomach and ribcage with every breath. My saxophone teacher told me many years ago not to worry about trying to hold my stomach in to look slim if I wanted to make a decent noise!
- Think of situations when you have felt particularly stressed. You might have felt tension in your throat or shoulders and have found yourself breathing rapidly. Is there a pattern of "trigger" situations that cause you to feel overwhelmed? If there is an obvious scenario that you can identify, take note of it and be prepared to apply your diaphragmatic breathing next time that you are in that situation.
- Caught yourself in a moment of overwhelm and stress? Follow these steps to calm the body and mind and regain clarity of focus:
    1. Step away from the scene. Remove yourself from the physical location where you are feeling stressed – even if just to walk around the corner.

2. Expand your ribcage and take a 7 second breath in through your nose. Hold for 7 seconds then release through your mouth for 7 seconds.
3. Repeat for at least a minute, focusing on counting the seconds, until you can feel that your stress levels have dropped and you are feeling calmer.
4. Reconsider the situation that you were in. What is the very first task that you should apply yourself to get through it?
5. Prioritise that in your thinking, then go back and focus *only* on that task until it is completed.

SECTION 2

PHYSICAL ENVIRONMENT HACKS

"Clearing the clutter in your physical space will go a long way toward clearing the clutter in your mind."

PETER WALSH

HACK #4
Clear the Clutter!

Have you ever wondered just *why* you have so many socks, when you are scrambling around in hurry to leave the house but can't find a matching pair? Or scratched your head in bewilderment over the clutter that has accumulated overnight on your office desk? It's times like these that one finds themselves seriously considering becoming a minimalist.

Minimalism is on trend at the moment, with minimalist rock stars such as Marie Kondo becoming household names. There is much to be said about the positive effects of this movement, as clutter is often a physical representation of the state of a person's mind. Too much mental or physical clutter can lead to procrastination, depression and low productivity.

In his book *Learning and Leading with Habits of Mind*, Arthur L.Costa discusses how the brain absorbs information through *all* of the senses, not just visually and aurally.[5] We tend to forget that our senses of smell, taste and touch are also information pathways to the brain. This ability to gather information in so many differing ways is an incredible gift, however can potentially be problematic too as we also have a variety of sources for potential distraction and reduced productivity.

Who knows a teenager whose bedroom resembles a bombsite? You may even have been this teenager in days gone by (sorry Mom!) Their wardrobe has exploded over the floor, amongst which are buried schoolbooks, shoes, chocolate wrappers, bags and last week's homework. This same teen is the one who can never remember anything and has a meltdown when they can't find their favourite top to wear to a party on the weekend.

Clutter is time-consuming, distracting, overwhelming, embarrassing, frustrating and productivity-destroying. A cluttered environment and mind is not going to support someone who aspires to live a rocking, on-purpose life!

So what does your present-day workplace look like? Is it overflowing with post-it notes, pens and broken pencils, correspondence, planners, photos, paper clips and other stationary items, ornaments, photos, phones, iPads, laptops and associated chargers and accessories?

How's that working for you?

The minute you pause from the task that you are immersed in, you run the risk of sensory overload in a cluttered workspace. Each one of your senses will be bombarded by information from your cluttered environment and your chances of remaining focused and productive will dramatically decrease.

How about your computer? Does it have a dozen tabs open and a desktop full of items that should be deleted or filed?

What does your smartphone look like? Are there pages and pages of apps that could be grouped into files so that you don't need to keep swiping away having to search every time that you want a particular app?

While we are at it, how is the rest of your home? Do you have a pantry full of out-of-date food and overflowing with plastic containers? Do you have drawers stuffed full of paperwork needing sorting? Is your linen cupboard set to explode with bedding that you don't no longer need?

Every one of these scenarios will contribute to a sensory overload that can negatively affect your focus and productivity. Even though you might work from a perfectly ordered office, coming home to a cluttered home is still going to raise your stress levels and hurt your productivity.

ACTION TASKS:

- In a nutshell – clear the clutter! Begin with your desk. Remove everything bar the basics from the surface. Continue with the rest of the room. Be ruthless! You want your work zone to be clear and to create the lowest sensory stimulation possible.
- Working one zone at a time, even if only for 15 minutes a day, tackle the other areas in your home or on your devices. Donate anything that you do not regularly use. It's time to clear that space in your home and in your head!
- Once you have decluttered your environment, make a commitment to yourself to recreate this clear space at the conclusion of every day. Begin this habit with your desk and extend it to your kitchen, bathroom and living spaces. Doing so will set you up for focused, productive work the next day.

Now put the book down and start clearing!

HACK #5

Ditch the Open-Space Office

How does your productivity fare in the workplace, in particular in an open-space workplace? Even the most extroverted person is going to find their productivity negatively affected when there are conversations happening nearby, a person coughing persistently across the room, the smell of your colleague's curry lunch and the sound of his chewing echoing through the office.

Once touted as the most revolutionary means of building a team in the workplace, open-space offices have been in vogue for many years. However, subsequent research has revealed that they are actually *not* conducive to high employee morale or productivity with studies showing that the noise levels and lack of privacy actually contribute to distraction, stress and demotivation.[6] Hardly supportive to achieving your goals and rocking your life!

A recent study conducted by researchers at the Harvard Business School confirmed this negative impact. After collecting data from two Fortune 500 companies who had embraced the open-space office layout, they discovered that instead of employees interacting more, the reverse actually occurred as people withdrew from one another and reverted to increased emailing and messaging to communicate.[7]

I've personally experienced the awkwardness of trying to talk to a coaching client in a large, echoing open-space office where our voices carried and we were conscious of others hearing our conversation. I've also had others tell me how lack of privacy negatively affected their phone calls to clients, particularly when delicate matters were being discussed. It is hard to be creative, focused and productive when you are overhearing your colleague having an argument with his wife on the phone at the desk opposite, or having your neighbor swing their chair over every few minutes to check out what you are up to and compare notes.

Open-plan offices also lead to the distracting sensory overload that we discussed in our previous hack. Constant noise, visual stimuli of people, movement, clutter and color, smells of food, even kinesthetic stimuli of being bumped or slapped on the shoulder in passing are all interruptions to our mental train of thought. Once that train is disrupted, it is hard to get it back on track and regain focus. The harder the task is that you are trying to work on, the less chance you have of completing it to a high standard if your environment is constantly working against you.

The same is true for the at-home worker who doesn't have their own separate office space to work in. Spouses, children, pets and even appliances all have the ability to cause those breaks in concentration that make completing your work feel like you are wading through mud.

ACTION TASKS:

- If you don't have control over the office plan in your workspace, talk to the person who does about the possibility of having private "quiet zones" installed where you can work privately and with minimal distractions.
- Unable to relocate your workspace? Utilize tools to cut down the sensory overload such as using noise-reducing headphones while you are working on tasks that require concentration. Your colleagues will soon learn not to interrupt you when your headphones are on.
- If working from home, spend a weekend setting up a private workspace that removes you from the noise and distractions of the main household. If you don't have an actual room available, get creative! Perhaps the conversion of a closet could provide you a workspace.
- Encourage your family to leave you alone when you are in your work zone.

HACK #6
Block the Noise!

Noise is a huge contributor to lack of productivity, and it is something that we are bombarded with constantly. You can actually grow used to certain levels which might bother other people. I experience this myself whenever I visit my parents in Sydney, Australia. They live near a busy road and the noise constantly bothers me, given that I live in a semi-rural area in Auckland, New Zealand, where I rarely hear traffic. It bothers me so much that I struggle to function, whereas my parents are so used to the noise that they don't even register it.

As already touched upon, noise is one of the huge negative factors of open-plan offices. In fact, research has revealed that if you can hear someone talking when you are trying to read or write, your productivity can drop by up to 66%! Whether you are a manager of employees or a solo entrepreneur trying to find the most efficient location to get your work done, this has got to be a sobering statistic. How will you ever stop procrastinating, focus and get that thing done when you are operating 66% less productively than usual?[8]

Noise pollution has been linked to the appearance of higher stress hormones in the body, rampant hearing loss across populations, and even delayed reading comprehension in children.[9] In a nutshell, even though we might not always be aware of it, sound has the potential to affect our thinking, emotions and behaviour.[10] Be it someone else's conversation, the pings of notifications or calls on our phones, overhead airplanes, traffic noise, loud music, or indeed, *any* music, all affect our physical body immediately. Our heart rates and rhythms all react to noise and our nervous system is particularly assaulted, which can lead to raised stress hormones and hypertension.

We need to manage the noise we are exposed to if we are to truly be focused and productively doing that thing that we want to do in order to live our lives on-purpose.

ACTION TASKS:

- I mentioned using noise-cancelling headphones earlier, and this is a great starting point, helping you get the silence that you need to be able to focus on task. Ensure that you are using headphones and not ear buds if listening to music however. Ear buds have been associated with hearing damage due to their location in the ear canal, which can raise levels up to nine decibels louder.
- Playing music through your headphones might seem a great way to distract from environmental noise, however it too can inhibit cognitive focus and recall, particularly if too loud and also if there are lyrics. An alternative is to try Binaural beats – music that researchers believe can activate specific brain systems according to which frequency pattern is used. The most popular pattern that is said to promote alertness and concentration is the Beta Pattern, set a frequency of 14-100Hz. A free, online sample of a Beta Pattern Binaural beat can be found here: https://www.youtube.com/watch?v=fxB82OvGEGo[11]
- Still struggling with noise distraction? Try an app to generate white noise through your headphones. There are plenty available and these will help mask background noises that break your concentration and prevent you doing that thing that you want to do.

SECTION 3

HEALTH AND WELLBEING HACKS

"It is well to be up before daybreak, for such habits contribute to health, wealth, and wisdom."

~ ARISTOTLE

HACK #7
Ditch the Snooze Button!

When I worked as a personal trainer, there were many times that I found myself alone at the gym at 5 am. Not intentionally alone mind you, rather, I had been stood-up by the client who had booked a session for that time. The usual reason for leaving me standing there? The alarm had gone off and they had pressed snooze again and again until it was too late.

Don't get me wrong – I didn't exactly *enjoy* getting up at 3.45 am every morning to be there ready for that client. However, I did it successfully, year in and year out. How? I learned very early in my PT career that hitting the snooze button was the death knell for getting out the door on time.

We all know that getting enough quality sleep is essential for optimal health and productivity. If you are suffering from lack of sleep, your brain is going to be sluggish, your immune system is compromised and you will generally feel like you are not functioning effectively. Quite frankly, you are going to feel like crap.

Good sleep hygiene is a must if you are to be in peak condition so that you can *rock* your life and do that thing you've been wanting to do. This starts with getting up at the same time every morning, which is why hitting that snooze button can derail your entire day. You are waking up yet wanting to sleep and the result is an uncomfortable drowsy and disoriented state called sleep inertia.[12] Instead of refreshing you like deep sleep does, those few minutes between each snooze alarm are confusing your body and brain, and ultimately causing you to feel more groggy. This grogginess or sleep inertia can affect you for hours afterwards and all of those goals you were intending smashing out that day will probably still be sitting there uncompleted come 5 pm.

Breaking the snooze button habit is the same as breaking any other negative habit in your life:

1. You need to *decide* that you are going to change things.
2. You need to *determine* what action you are going to implement instead – in this case, getting out of bed straight away.
3. You need to set up your environment to *support* this outcome.
4. You need to apply some tough-love *self discipline* and push through these actions again and again until the new habit is automatic.

What is the ultimate outcome that you are wanting here? To be refreshed, alert and feeling great so that you can tackle the goals and tasks that you need and want to do to live your life on-purpose. Right? Then decide today that you are going to proactively put a sleep habit into place that will support the life that you want to live!

ACTION TASKS:

Set yourself up for sleep success by establishing good habits BEFORE you even get into bed:

- Have a regular bedtime.
- Stop all screen time an hour before bed, or at least consider yellow lenses to block the effect of the blue light of your phone, which has been linked to the suppression of the production of melatonin, the hormone that influences circadian rhythms.[13]
- Sleep in a cool room. Studies have shown that in order for the body to lower its core temperature and cycle through the sleep stages, the optimal room temperature should be between 15–19 degrees (60–67 degrees Fahrenheit). Too warm and you will find your sleep broken as your core struggles to cool down. In my case, I have a fan or air-conditioning on all year around as it keeps me cool and provides the white noise I need to mask household noises which break my sleep (let's just say too that air-conditioning is a menopausal woman's best friend!).[14]
- Have complete darkness in your room. Failing that, wear a sleep mask. Any light, particularly the blue light of a digital clock or cell phone, has the ability to disrupt your sleep cycles.
- Determine that you will *not* push that snooze button! If it is a separate button on your clock, tape it over or disable it. Otherwise, place the alarm device over the other side of the room so that you need to actually get out of bed to go and turn it off. Once you are up,

you are up! Resist the urge to get back into that bed and you will be well on your way to feeling more alert and focused and *rocking* your life!

HACK #8

Move that Body!

> "Leave all the afternoon for exercise and recreation, which are as necessary as reading. I will rather say more necessary because health is worth more than learning".
>
> ~ THOMAS JEFFERSON

We all know that exercise is good for the body. It helps us stay healthy, keeps us strong, keeps us supple, lifts our mood, positively affects our blood pressure and helps our brains work more efficiently.

So why do so many of us make every excuse under the sun to not exercise?

Despite knowing how important exercise is for our health and wellbeing, it is generally the first thing we ditch when we are immersed in a project or overwhelmed with everything else that we are juggling in life. I've certainly been guilty of neglecting to exercise at times in my life.

However, I've also experienced the sensation of how good I feel when I *do* exercise regularly. Trust me when I say that the difference in how I feel when I do find the time to exercise as compared to when I don't is significant.

If you are really wanting to *rock* your life and operate at peak productivity, exercise needs to become an essential part of your daily routine. Really, it's up there with sleeping well, eating well and drinking enough water. But where to start? Especially when you have neglected doing anything for a while?

Being a qualified personal trainer, my preference is that strength training is the gold standard for everyone, regardless of gender or age. Women need to build muscle just as much as men do and given our hormonal make-up, it is far harder for us to do so and far easier for us to lose muscle mass rapidly if we neglect it, hence the need to incorporate strength training regularly.

Working with all sorts of different people over the years has taught me that the best way to introduce exercise into non-exercisers' lives was to find something that they enjoy. While many were open and happy to join me on the weights floor from the get-go, many others needed to be eased into the routine of regular exercise. Be it regular walking or hiking, dancing or team sports, those who enjoyed what they were doing were the ones who ultimately not only stuck at their exercise routine, but were then open to trying new things as well.

No idea of where to start? Harvard Medical School has a great list of what they consider to be five of the best

exercises that you can do, regardless of your fitness level.[15] They are:
- Swimming
- Tai chi
- Strength Training
- Walking
- Kegel exercises

If you can change your perception of exercise being something that you *have* to do, to something that you *want* to do, you will find that half the battle is won right there. Add in the bonus of the endorphins release triggered by exercise – you will be feeling on top of the world in no time!

ACTION TASKS:

- When you are planning your schedule for the following week, schedule exercise into your diary. Give it the same weight of importance as any other meeting and determine to keep your word to yourself that you will follow through. While some people prefer to schedule their session early in the morning before their day begins, others find that their schedule works better when they incorporate exercise later in the day. Find out what works for you and stick to it!
- Book that personal training session, swimming lesson or private tai chi lesson. The biggest inhibitor to people getting started with an exercise program is fear of the unknown. Not knowing how systems work in the gym, not knowing how to use the equipment or embarrassing yourself by doing the wrong moves in a class can be such an inhibitor to sticking with exercise. Counter this from the get-go by booking an appointment with a trainer or instructor who can help you feel more comfortable with not only how to exercise safely and effectively, but also familiarize you with the surrounds of the space you will be exercising in.
- Have your gym gear packed and ready to go the night before. Speaking from personal experience, there is nothing worse than staggering around at 3.45 am looking for a clean pair of socks. Having your gym gear sorted, packed and ready to either put on or take

with you, will make sticking to your commitment to exercise so much more achievable. I have dozens of former clients who will testify to the fact that doing this simple act, along with not pressing snooze anymore, totally changed their lives in regards to exercising regularly.

HACK #9
Nourish Yourself!

Ever had a night out where you ate all the processed food you could think of, then felt sluggish and hungover for the next few days? Or been on holiday where you ate take-away for days on end until you found yourself craving simple, wholesome food that you could prepare for yourself?

It is a no-brainer in this information age that good nutrition is paramount to good health. It directly affects so many of the body's systems, helps prevent certain diseases such as Type-2 Diabetes and also plays a crucial part in keeping your brain healthy, which is critical if you are to do that thing you are wanting to achieve and *rock* your life.

There are numerous studies available linking nutrition to cognitive function, with many focusing on the Mediterranean Diet.[16]

This diet is high in fats and fruits that contribute to the fatty acids and polyphenols which studies have demonstrated can support healthy cognitive function while also potentially slowing down the onset of age-related diseases like Alzheimers.

There is a plethora of specialist information available about nutrition, so we are just touching on the topic here by acknowledging its impact on our wellbeing and productivity. It is an area that cannot be neglected though. If you are truly wishing to operate in your most optimal state, you need to do your utmost to ensure that your body and brain is getting the fuel it needs to function well and the starting point that I always recommended to my gym clients is including protein at every meal.

Unlike the other macronutrients of carbohydrates and fats, there are no large protein stores in the body so this nutrient needs to be replenished regularly. Protein is also crucial as it contains the essential amino acids needed by the body to function including transporting vitamins and minerals around the body and balancing body fluids. Adequate protein intake can also help you maintain muscle mass which also affects how your body metabolizes food. It can help manage your appetite, being more satiating and support your immune system and general wellbeing.

If needing a guide to determine approximately how much protein to include in your diet, the easiest way to plan for your specific needs is to book an appointment with a registered dietician. As well, general guidelines for protein intake, along with other nutrients can be found in the free downloadable booklet "Nutrient Reference Values for Australia and New Zealand" available from the

New Zealand Ministry of Health website. (http://www.moh.govt.nz)[17]

We impact our wellbeing and our ability to function at our best when our nutrition is below par, yet even though most of us understand this, we still struggle to eat in a way that supports us as we pursue our goals. Even more confusingly, we eat food when we are not actually hungry, using it as a means to distract ourselves and procrastinate when we really should be getting stuck in and focusing on what we are trying to achieve. It's time to remove the complicated rules, diets and negative emotions around food and simplify how we eat so that we can get on with *rocking* our lives – healthy and happy!

ACTION TASKS:

- Protein first! At every meal, include a palm sized portion of protein. There are so many choices! Meat, chicken, fish, eggs, tofu. Your body will thank you for it and you'll find that you feel more satisfied after every meal.
- Include more walnuts, berries and fatty fish like salmon in your diet. Studies have shown that fatty acids as found in the fish and the walnuts, along with the polyphenols found in berries, have been found to positively affect cognitive function.[18]
- Choose foods in their natural, unprocessed states. Artificial colors, sweeteners and chemical preservatives are detrimental to health and should largely be shunned if you are wanting to support your body and brain. Most of us enjoy a treat from time to time, however if you can at least adhere to the 80/20 principle of 80% healthy whole food and 20% or less of "treat" food, you will be setting yourself up for overall better health. Not sure where to start and overwhelmed with all of the diet plans out there? Consider meeting with a nutritionist to set up an eating plan personalized for you.
- Do you feel like food has become your procrastination outlet, or that you have lost control over portion sizes? It is easy to substitute hard work with avoidance activities like raiding the fridge, especially if you work from home. I talk from experience here! If you know that food has become an issue and you

are eating for reasons other than to actually nourish your body and brain, take the initiative and implement some behavior modification techniques that address your specific situation. To do this however, you'll need to begin by removing the denial sunglasses in order to identify the specific areas that you struggle with. Once you have "owned up," you can then come up with some creative strategies to break those negative habits.

Some simple examples might be: substituting sparkling mineral water for your regular soda fix; scheduling a walk or an exercise session at that time of day when you would routinely leave work and head straight to the nearest fast food outlet; changing your route to and from work if you are tempted by the hot donut shops on the way and taking the time to chew your food a certain amount of times to break your habit of woofing down huge portions mindlessly.

Removing both the behavior and the associated feelings of guilt and shame will free you up to truly focus on doing that thing you *want* to do with your life.

HACK #10
Drink that Water!

"Yeah, yeah," I hear you say. We all know that we should drink approximately eight cups a day, but do you actually do it?

And why the big deal?

Unfortunately, not many of us do actually drink enough water. Instead, we fill up with cups of coffee, which is actually a mild diuretic, sodas, which are full of chemicals and sugar, and our bodies end up actually being dehydrated.

There have been numerous studies linking dehydration of just 2% or more to an increased perception of fatigue, mood disruption and even the impairment of cognitive functions like memory and the ability to concentrate. In fact, cognitive performance such as short-term memory, your mood and your visual attention are all directly affected by severe dehydration.[19] These are not things you want your body to be wrestling with when you are trying to focus on what you need to do to achieve your goal!

The body generally loses approximately 4% of bodyweight in water a day, and the broad guidelines of 8 × 250ml cups for women and 10 for men helps meet this loss. Too much water can strip your minerals and electrolytes however, which is why some folks recommend adding a pinch of Celtic sea salt to your water to replenish these vital elements, rather than reaching for one of those highly promoted chemical cocktails advertised as electrolyte drinks. The condition of Hyponatremia which refers to low blood sodium is what we see occur in some high performance athletes who have competed in gruelling, long marathons where their sodium levels were severely depleted.

When you find yourself distracted and losing focus during the day, it's worth pausing to ask yourself if you are simply thirsty. How many times have you reached for a sugary snack or a caffeine fix when you were actually slightly dehydrated? A glass of water might be all you need to help you regain focus and get back on track with working towards your goal.

ACTION TASKS:

- Measure out a 250 ml glass then keep a tally in your daily diary of how many of these are consumed.
- Grab yourself a large glass or aluminium drinking bottle when leaving the house and measure how many of these you should be drinking. Again, keep a tally in your diary.
- Keep your bottle handy when in the car or in your office.
- Purchase some Celtic sea salt and add a teaspoon to each bottle or a pinch to each glass and while you are at it – throw away any energy drinks or sports drinks that you might have still stashed in your pantry!
- Feeling thirsty? Drink up!
- Feeling tired, distracted or reaching aimlessly for the cookie jar? Drink your water!
- Working physically on a hot day or exercising vigorously? Increase your water intake.

SECTION 4

TIME HACKS

"Time is the scarcest resource and unless it is managed nothing else can be managed."

~ PETER DRUCKER

"Time is at once the most valuable and the most perishable of all our possessions."

~ JOHN RANDOLPH

HACK #11
Clear the Forest so You Can See the Trees

If only I had a dollar for every occasion that I bewailed not having "enough time"! "Managing" time has become an industry in itself over the past few decades, with companies vying to produce the most effective and complex planning systems, both paper and digital, with the intention of helping us all become far more adept at making every moment count.

Yet how many of us begin the use of our planners with great enthusiasm, only for them to peter out around month four? Or, regardless of how much we have invested in the latest planning system, we still default to trying to keep important dates in our heads?

Time management is such a critical key to us getting that thing done that we want to achieve. Without the deep comprehension that time really is fleeting, we allow ourselves to fritter it away and find ourselves at the end of each week wondering what on earth we actually did over those previous five days.[20] This is certainly no way to *rock* our life!

Let's get real though: having an issue with "time-management" is sugar-coating the fact that you really have an issue with "self-management." Right? In fact, feeling like there is never enough time generally reflects one or many states that you might be in including the biggie – the state of overwhelm.

Ever felt paralyzed by the sheer amount of work that you need to get done, so much so that you end up filling in your time with "busyness" but actually have nothing definitive to show for it at the end of the week?

Or found yourself zoning out in front of Netflix when you know that you have a backlog of work needing to be done?

Or even found yourself suddenly deciding to declutter your wardrobe while the book that you have been wanting to write forever remains at chapter one on your computer in the other room?

These are all symptoms of a mind that is in a state of overwhelm, where the sheer volume of things to do have become so great in number that your subconscious has now identified them as being negative and harmful to you. Your brain is now trying to protect you by distracting you with the need to take on easy, less stressful tasks instead and failure to recognise this and take alternative action will mean that you end up stuck. Stuck not knowing how to break out of the rut you suddenly feel you are in and stuck feeling like an imposter who is not capable or worthy of achieving the dream you want to achieve.

Learning how to prioritise the multitude of tasks that are overwhelming you is the first step in taking back control of all of the "must-do's" that are swamping your life and affecting your emotions. Once you have mastered the ability to identify, categorise, prioritise and schedule your tasks – you will find that your heightened stress levels begin to subside as you are able to move forward towards the achievement of your goal. What is also exciting is that once you have mastered this process, you will be able to apply it in so many other areas of your life where you feel weighed down and overwhelmed by tasks. Be it in the workplace or at home, having the skill to par back the sheer volume of things needing doing to reveal those that are the most important will make a huge difference to your ability to truly focus on those things that matter. All part of living your life *On*-purpose.

ACTION TASKS

- A very easy way of thinning the forest of all of the needs, must-dos and responsibilities is to take some time on your own and do a brain dump of every single item that is weighing on you. Write it all down! This act alone will make such a huge difference to your psyche in that you are actually acknowledging all the things that have been festering in your brain.
- Use different colored pencils to shade or circle related items. For example, you might have a number of tasks to do with your home maintenance. Ring these in green. You might have a number of health checks needing to be booked (dentist, optometrist, etc.). Circle these in blue – you get the idea.
- Now choose the most urgent task from each grouping and list these on a new page.
- Pull out your diary. Allocate a time for each of these most urgent tasks over the next week, ONLY ALLOCATING ONE TASK A DAY.
- Honor these appointments in the same way that you would honor an appointment with your boss. As they are completed, actively tick them off.
- At the end of the week, check which of the tasks were completely done, reschedule those which need another appointment and add one or two of the next level of urgent choices from your master list. This way you will be taking action on your master list while

removing the overwhelm and procrastination that comes from the enormity of so many tasks.
- Celebrate at the end of the week when tasks can be completely removed from your master list!

HACK #12
Map Your Wheel of Life

"The key is not to prioritize what's on your schedule, but to schedule your priorities."

~ STEPHEN COVEY

Have you ever sat down and decided what your priorities in life actually are, or do you find that you always feel like you are in constant crisis management? Having to deal with whatever is thrown at you in any particular moment and never getting on and making any headway in what you *really* want to be achieving?

You might have done the huge brain dump of Hack #11 and discovered some key tasks that need to be seen to. However, while you know that you really need to get a dental check-up, you more urgently need to fix the leak in your roof and complete the report that your boss is waiting on.

How do you work out where to begin and how to prioritise your time and energy?

Before starting any coaching, I generally get clients to complete a Wheel of Life exercise. Originally created by Zig Ziglar, the Wheel of Life is a visual representation of the key areas that most people have to deal with in their lives. The most common version has eight categories, though you can adapt the wheel concept to suit whatever areas that you want. The idea is to ask yourself numerous questions associated with that category then give yourself a rating.

Once you have all sections completed, you will have eight ratings, with lower ratings representing a life area that is being more neglected than an area rating higher. This way, you can see visually where your time and attention are being focused.

For instance, you may rate yourself as going reasonably well in the areas of finance and personal development, lower in the areas of romance / relationships and health and extremely low in the recreation section.

Imagine the person who has been feeling a bit short-tempered and "off" for a while, walking around feeling like life had lost its sheen, and they are presented with these findings in a visual context? Immediately they can see the areas that have been lacking in their life. From this awareness, they can then move on to goal setting, decision making and, most importantly, taking back ownership of where they choose to use their time!

Before you head into the Action steps, grab a piece of paper and draw a large circle, then divide this circle into 8 segments. Label these segments with the following names:

1. Romance
2. Recreation
3. Career
4. Personal Development
5. Finances
6. Health
7. Environment
8. Relationships

As you move through the following guide questions for the segments, place a dot in the middle of each segment to represent your rating. If the dot is near the centre of the wheel, the rating is low. If the dot is near the circle edge, the rating is high. When finished, colour in each segment to give a solid visual picture of the areas of your life that are rocking and those that could use some more love.

ACTION TASKS:

▶ Fill out your own Wheel of Life. Get creative and use different colors for each segment as you rate them. Here are the categories along with some prompting questions that you can ask yourself:

Environment: where you live and where you work. Are you in the midst of the city with all of its noise and bustle? In the suburbs? Near the beach or in a rural setting? Is your work environment stimulating, oppressive or neutral? How does your environment make you feel? Is it conducive to you achieving the things that you want to achieve?

Career: are you working in a field that interests you or do you want to change completely? Are you satisfied with your earnings, your potential for development, your co-workers, your boss?

Finances: are you earning enough to survive? Are you struggling? Have you got limiting beliefs around money that hold you back? Are you unsure of how to invest your money? Are you wanting to earn more?

Health: how are you feeling energetically? Are you eating/sleeping/hydrating well? Are you moving your body and participating in resistance training? Are you having regular wellness and dental check-ups?

Relationships: do you make time to socialize with your family and friends? Are there relationships that you have let slip and want to repair? Have you been so busy that you feel lonely?

Romance: are you wanting to find a partner but don't have the time? Is your relationship with your partner strong or have you been neglecting it?

Personal Development: are you the same person you were ten years ago or have you grown in outlook, thinking and achievement? Do you make time to read, learn and study? Have you undertaken any new classes, be they academic, physical or artistic, to continue your personal development?

Recreation: do you take time for regular social outings? Do you book regular holidays? Do you allow time for hobbies and fun activities?

- Identify your top three strongest categories and have a think about what is going well with those areas. Are they things that can be maintained with less time?
- Identify your lowest three categories and write down three things that you could implement to raise the rating of this area in your life.
- Take the most significant idea from each of these categories and list them on a separate page of paper.

- ▶ These top three items are now the most critical priorities that need to be addressed for you to see improvement in these lagging areas of your life. Now you have identified them, you can prioritize them in your scheduling, get that thing done that you've been wanting to do and ROCK your life!

HACK #13

Knock Off the Hard Stuff First!

I've heard many different time-management folks rave about what works for them. They get you so excited at the possibility that theirs is the gospel that will solve your time-management woes that you end up purchasing all of their books and systems to teach you to imitate them. They all seem to have their pet themes: "Don't consume before you create," "journal first before anything," "don't answer emails or check social media before noon," "exercise before you work," and so on.

All of these tips have merit and I have personally tried each and every one of them at some stage (just like I've tried every diet under the sun!)

I can guarantee that if you are anything like me, you tend to run to extremes. If I have decided that I am not going to respond to social media or email prior to noon, and then I inadvertently catch a message notification that is urgent and respond to it, I subconsciously grade myself as "failed" and this affects my performance over the rest of the day. In reality, the more black and white rules I establish with my time-management, the more I set myself up for failure.

For instance, let's look at the reality of the "no social media and email before midday" rule. I run three online community groups as well as a large business page and various other social media channels through which I connect to and communicate with my audience. I'm also based in New Zealand, which means that a lot of action in these groups takes place during my sleep hours. I find that I can't focus on my work for the day until I have checked what is happening across my groups.

What if there has been an argument in the group overnight that has caused members to leave? What if someone has decided to spam all the members? What if a member has reached out with a vulnerable message that requires a reply? The "no checking social media before midday" rule just doesn't work for me. On the other hand, we all know what a rabbit hole that social media can be and how much time can be wasted scrolling and commenting, so instead, I limit myself to an hour every morning to cover all of my groups, answering messages, checking member posts, and also checking my email accounts. Here, I delete any spam and highlight anything that I will need to respond to later in the day. Following this morning routine, social media channels are hidden and I am focused on my work.

In this case, I applied the principle instead of the rule in regards to no social media before midday. My situation is such that I feel that I do need to check in on my channels and mail before doing any work. However, I restrict that time and adhere to the principle of not letting social media distract me from my prioritized tasks by shutting it down immediately after checking.

Life happens and it is very rare that two days are ever the same. If we bind ourselves up with rules, we set ourselves up to be failures, and who wants to work like that? Better to grab the principle behind a rule that does carry merit and apply it to your life to better your productivity. If you can't exercise first thing in the morning, simply make sure that you exercise *somewhere* during your day and I still advocate you locking it in your diary so that it is a daily priority. I've been finding lately that if I am working and writing at home for an entire day, I actually don't want to get in a car and lose a few hours going to the gym, so prefer to do shorter bursts of exercise in and around my work at home. Being flexible in my thinking means that I don't then beat myself up for not going to the gym, but instead stick to the principle of daily exercise by doing something at home.

Another rule that always challenged me is the "tick the five hardest things off your list before 10 am" rule. I love the concept as I am certainly one of the world's biggest procrastinators when it comes to doing "hard things". (Which in this introvert's case, generally relates to phone calls. I will do housework for hours to avoid making calls!) However, trying to implement this rule has often felt like trying to start one of the many diets I've inflicted on myself over the years. Exciting at first – this was going to be the thing to change my life – followed by those fabulous first few days where I proudly ticked the five things off my list. Then something happened and I had to race a cat to the vet, or an appointment went over time, etc. and soon I no longer had a series of five ticks on every day of my diary, just sporadic ticks here and there.

And then I gave up on it altogether, counting myself a useless failure.

Again.

Instead, I now use the *principle* of this rule to help me "get that hard thing done" every day. Whatever the prioritized task is for the day, my general principal is to get it done first! This means that after I have done my morning check of all groups/channels/emails, I sit down and face the hardest task for the day. "Hardest" may not be something that is particularly challenging to do, but is a task that I feel any sense of resistance towards.

What's "hard" for you? For me, writing falls into this category. I actually love writing and once I am in the zone, I can get lost in the process. Getting started however, is a whole other issue. I will find myself doing admin work, playing with graphics, cleaning my wardrobe out, inspecting my teeth in the mirror ... all part of my procrastination repertoire to avoid doing something that will require focus and effort.

Ironic, isn't it? If I set myself a black and white rule that says "no social media before writing and all writing has to be done before 11 am", I set myself up to fail. If instead I say, "do your hard thing first" (after my morning routine of social media check in), I set myself up to win.

"But what if you have more than one 'hard thing'?" I hear you ask. This is where your prioritizing comes into play. I personally have a few "hard things" that are part of my business, so not only do I do them first, but I prioritize them over different days of the week so that all of them at some stage are the first focus of the day.

ACTION TASKS:

- Out of the tasks that you need to complete (and these don't have to be just work-related), list the ones that you consider to be "hard things".
- Prioritize the order of these tasks according to urgency, then schedule them out over your week accordingly. For instance, a trip to the dentist might be scheduled on a weekend rather than a workday. A phone call to discuss your overdraft with your bank manager would be considered more urgent than planning your birthday invitation list.
- Pat yourself on the back every time that you complete your "hard thing" first up in the day!

HACK #14
Use a Timer!

There are many schools of thought of time-management that promote the concept of working in short, focused blocks of time. Doing so gives you a greater chance on focusing on the task at hand, being less susceptible to distractions and ultimately getting more done. Who doesn't want those results?

One of the more popular and easily applicable techniques is the well-known Pomodoro Techinique, and it is such an easily applied productivity technique that can be applied directly or adapted and personalised to suit anyone's needs.

Created in the 1980s by Francesco Cirillo, this technique, named "Pomodoro", Italian for tomato, after the tomato-shaped timer he personally used, requires a timer to be set for 25 minutes, during which you set the intention to commit 100% focus to the task at hand. Once the timer goes off, you have a short break then reset it. After you have completed 3–4 25minute blocks, you then have a longer break.[21]

As simple as it sounds, this technique really does work well as anyone can commit to "just" 25 minutes of focused activity – right? You are simply bargaining with yourself. "If I write this blog post for the next 25 minutes, I can have a break and make a hot chocolate." Given that the time blocks are so short, you are setting yourself up for success. Repeated success is not only going to get your task completed, but will build up your confidence and self-belief along the way.

Winning!

Even better though, is that by adopting the "principle not the rule" attitude that I referred to earlier, you can take this concept of working in short, focused blocks of time and modify it to suit your own style and circumstances. I have personally come up with my own method of work energy cycling, combining my knowledge of personal training techniques with time-management methods such as the Pomodoro Technique.

Let me explain: are you someone who *really* struggles at the moment with focus? I would suggest that you begin with shorter blocks of 20 minutes. You could intersperse these with longer intervals of less focused activity that are still directly related to the project you are working on, then cycle these high intensity / lower intensity sessions until you have completed your task goal for the day. I liken this to HIIT (high intensity interval training) exercise programs where clients alternate short bursts of intense physical exercise, designed to raise their heart rates and challenge their cardio-vascular systems, with less intensive phases where their heart rates are able to lower again. For instance you might aim to complete 1–2 high energy client calls in that first 20 minutes, followed by 30 minutes of lower energy client - related paperwork. Then you might take a 5–10 minute break to refill your drink bottle and have a stretch before launching into your next 20 minute high energy block of client calls.

Perhaps you find that you need longer to really get stuck into your task? You might opt for 40 minute focused blocks with a 5 minute time out at the conclusion, before beginning the following 50 minute block. The first 40 minutes would require higher energy input, the following 50, a lower level. Find yourself a unique song or alarm that you can use to keep you on track with your time – particularly your breaks – and you will find that this self-applied HIIW – *high intensity interval working* – technique soon becomes second nature. You'll also find that you are steadily conquering those tasks that move you towards reaching your goals.

Be warned however, setting a timer is still not going to stop the producer of the greatest volume of your interruptions: your brain. While you can put your phone on silent and change your email settings to not send notifications to distract you and break your chain of thought – it is much harder to turn your brain off. I don't know about you, but I am constantly wrangling my thoughts to keep focused on the task that I am meant to be focused on. Even while writing this passage, I have found myself wondering what appointments I have this week, thinking about the calls

I need to make tomorrow, contemplating what I am going to cook for dinner tonight and musing over what a fabulous life my cats have who are sprawled alongside me as I tap away on my laptop. Not at all conducive to staying focused and "in the zone."

This battle with our brain is similar to another battle many of us are very used to. Ever been on a diet and the second that you were told that you couldn't eat something, all of a sudden it is all that you could think of? If we label our thoughts as "enemies" that we need to fight and subdue in order to stay on task – we will forever be in a no-win situation of beating ourselves up and feeling like failures. Certainly no way to *rock* your life! Instead, appreciate the fact that your brain is creative and clever and rather than wasting energy trying to suppress the thoughts, have a piece of paper next to your work station where you can write them down immediately. That way you can release them in the knowledge that you will address them in one of your upcoming breaks.

Finding your own unique High Intensity Interval Working method will not only help you break procrastination and *do* that thing – but will bring such a feeling of achievement and satisfaction as you increasingly improve your productivity and performance. And it all begins with getting yourself a timer!

ACTION TASKS:

- Find a unique sound to use for your timer bell on your phone, or purchase a fun kitchen timer.
- Have a notepad and pen on your desk next to your timer to write down the random thoughts that will try to distract you.
- Choose your main focus for the first half of the day, and create a list of the high energy tasks and low energy tasks associated with this focus.
- Choose the length of your high and low energy time blocks, set your timer and begin!
- At the conclusion of each block, use your designated break time between focus sessions to check through the list of random thoughts and add to your planner according to priority.
- Grab some water, have a stretch, reset that timer and get going again!

SECTION 5

ATTITUDE HACKS

"Ability is what you're capable of doing.
Motivation determines what you do.
Attitude determines how well you do it."

~ LOU HOLTZ

HACK #15
Find Your Pedestal

There have been a number of research studies investigating the links between procrastination and numerous human variables such as personality types, the desire for instant gratification, the addiction to the adrenaline rush of being under a time pressure, as well as many others. One such study titled "Academic procrastination of undergraduates: Low self-efficacy to self-regulate predicts higher levels of procrastination." even put the figures for university students experiencing chronic procrastination as high as 70–95%![22]

Procrastination affects just about everyone to some degree and even the person with the most exciting dream of living an on-purpose life is not immune to it. It seems crazy that we procrastinate when we so strongly desire to achieve something but so many of us do. We've already looked at some practical hacks to help break this negative habit, but there is another area of our life that significantly affects procrastination that we haven't yet addressed.

If we don't take the time to look at this area in our own lives, we will be always hampered in our attempts to do that thing we are wanting to do – regardless of what time-management techniques we apply.

This area is our own self-belief.

If you believe deep down that you are not worthy of achieving, you will subconsciously sabotage your progress, and procrastination is one of the most effective means of doing this. For instance, even though you pay lip service to wanting to complete a degree, you might subconsciously not feel that someone from your background deserves to do so. Chances are, if you don't address this inner belief, you will create a self-fulfilling prophecy and really *won't* succeed.

On the other hand, you might hold a secret inner belief that achieving your goal could make others in your family or circle feel less about themselves. The old adage of "you don't need to dim your light for others to shine brightly" exists because of this very belief. Women in particular can be so prone to subconsciously holding themselves back, not wanting to shine too brightly in case they draw the spotlight from their husbands, children or friends.

It seems silly to read in black and white, yet I know so many women who have defaulted to this inner wiring, like an internalizing of the tall poppy syndrome which affects the Kiwi and Aussie culture on so many levels. Best not be too high an achiever in case others notice and start to say you are "full of yourself!"

Then there is the inner belief regarding your self-efficacy. This is one area that has been particularly studied by researchers, as a person's self-efficacy has been found to directly affect their ability to perform well in any area in life.[23] Having a strong, positive self-efficacy means that you have the belief that you *can* actually achieve the goal that is in front of you.

If, deep down, you truly don't believe that you are capable of completing a task, you will fail to self-regulate your time and energy. Instead, you will self-hinder and ultimately self-sabotage your efforts to *do that thing*. As we've already pointed out, procrastination is one of the biggest weapons in your self-sabotage arsenal and you will find that it creeps more and more into your day when your core belief is that you actually do not have the skills or capability to complete the task you have undertaken.

To counter this, I'm declaring that it is time to put yourself on a pedestal!

Metaphorically speaking, of course.

In the same way that you put other people on pedestals – thinking that they are smarter, more talented, more worthy and more capable than you – it's time to put yourself on one too.

It's time to kick those inner lies to the curb. You ARE worthy of success and even if you don't yet have the skills, you ARE capable of learning what is needed in order to do that thing you are wanting to do and ROCK your life!

ACTION TASKS:

▶ Retrain your brain! Go back to the very first hack of this book – Visualization – and apply this same technique by creating a mental picture of yourself. This time, I want you to really focus on seeing yourself doing those steps and tasks that you need to master in order to do that thing and achieve that goal. This is the same technique that athletes do when they are trying to master a new skill. As an example, my daughter represented New Zealand numerous times as a junior aerobic gymnast, and she would do this practice of visualization not only prior to a competition where she would run her full routine mentally numerous times, but as part of the process of learning any new skills. Being able to picture herself completing the skill and "feeling" how the skill was meant to be executed not only meant that when it came time to attempt the skill physically, her body responded quickly, already knowing the pathway it needed to follow, but strengthened her self-efficacy – her belief that she *was* capable of mastering this task.

Likewise, when I was learning difficult passages of music when studying for exams for my music degree, I would picture the notes and feel the patterns in my fingers when commuting to and from the Conservatorium. My self-efficacy that I would master this piece of stage increased as I pictured myself performing it over and over.

- Decide to start speaking well of yourself. Whenever you feel yourself sliding into procrastination and thinking that you are not worthy of or good enough to do that thing, step away and apply the Breathe technique in Hack #3 then affirm to yourself verbally that you ARE capable of doing the task that you need to do.
- You've completed the above steps? Time to show a bit of tough love to yourself now. Sit your butt down and DO the thing! It might feel like you are wading through thick, sludgy mud getting going, but if you can keep reminding yourself that you *are* capable and worthy and you are definitely *not* giving up, you will find that your attitude and your procrastination habit will change. You will begin to enter a state where the sludgy mud sensation melts away as your creative juices begin to flow.

HACK #16
Establish Your Boundaries

Are you a people pleaser? Are you so busy trying to do what others want you to do that you don't seem to have the time or ability to focus on completing that thing that you say you *really* want to achieve?

If this is you, you are definitely not alone! Many people, women in particular, (yours truly included) fall into this trap. They find that they give so much of their time and head space to other people's needs that they not only struggle to achieve that thing they are *really* wanting to do, but they develop a festering resentment towards those other people and also towards themselves.

Having boundaries can feel selfish when you are used to putting other people's needs before your own. Even more so when the thing you are wanting to do is something new and special to you as it is something that you have never before achieved. How strange does it feel saying no to a friend who wants you to come hang out, when it is the only time that you had set aside to write, and you've never before ever written a book? It can feel wrong to let others down over something that you don't even know that you are capable of doing! The thing is though, if you truly want to achieve that goal and *rock* your life, you need to establish the boundaries needed to give yourself the space you need to bring it to fruition.

One of the presentations that I deliver as a professional speaker is called "Are you living your life in 3D?" and is about the voices in your world that have the ability to affect you and the choices you make for your life. One of the outside voices is the "Voice of Distraction." This is the voice that tells you that you should be doing any number of things *other* than that thing that you know deep down that you *should* be doing. These boundaries are critical too, as often this particular voice will come from a well meaning friend or family member who thinks that they are helping by suggesting that you follow their idea. It's these people who are the hardest to say no to.

It's well known that a plane that flies just one degree off course will end up in an entirely different location to the one that it was meant to be heading for. Listening to a "Voice of Distraction" has the ability to set you off your course and before you know it, you will find yourself nowhere near achieving the thing that you had wanted to achieve. Instead, you will be busy fulfilling someone else's agenda. As the saying goes, if you don't follow your own dreams, someone else will get you to follow theirs.

The way to prevent a "Voice of Distraction" from sending you off target is to have firm boundaries set in place. Boundaries that will help you stay on course. Boundaries that will help you protect the time, head space and focus you need in order to do the work YOU want to do.

Setting such boundaries can feel selfish, but they are you showing yourself self-care. You are showing yourself and others that you value your time, your feelings and your purpose. You are demonstrating to the world that YOU determine the agenda for your own life, not somebody else.

Healthy boundaries, as opposed to rigid, inflexible unhealthy ones where you are closed to anyone else's input and wisdom, are essential if you are to develop and maintain the laser focus you need to achieve the steps you need to work your way up in order to reach your goal.

Healthy boundaries mean that you are valuing your own goals and are able to stand on your own decisions. They also mean that you won't be swayed from your values or get caught up in other people's agendas, no matter how well-meaning they might sound.

ACTION TASKS:

- What are the "non-negotiable" priorities in your life? Time with your partner? Family? Completing your personal goal – that thing that you want to achieve? Write them down on a list, along with some ideas of what these non-negotiables look like in an average week. Some examples might be: an hour of chill out time every work night and an outing or date once a week with your partner. A family outing every weekend. An hour every second day to work on your book/your painting/your body at the gym.
- Schedule times for all of these non-negotiables over the next month. I still use a paper diary as well as an online one, and find that I am even clearer on how my week is looking when I use different colors for each type of time block.
- Stand your ground and protect these time blocks! Sometimes, there will be a valid reason for things changing, but this next month is the time for you to begin to flex those self-care, boundary-enforcing muscles.
- Once you have defined these time-focused boundaries, begin to look at other areas of your life. Where else have your let your boundaries be encroached? Is it in the workplace where you always seem to be picking up the slack for your co-workers? Is it in friendships where you feel like you are always dragged into other people's dramas?

- Make a list of areas in your life where you know that you need to put boundaries in place and make a resolve to start doing so, even if just working on one boundary at a time.

HACK #17
Choose Your Mood

In the Myers-Briggs method of assessing and understanding types of personalities, there is a particular distinction in thinking and behavior by which people are identified as "thinkers" or "feelers." Generally speaking, when making decisions, thinkers tend to be more rational and purposeful when they make decisions whereas feelers are often guided by emotions and personal preferences.[24]

I have one child who presents more strongly as a feeler. The other is more of a thinker. My husband and I are also both thinkers, although as I get older, I definitely see some feeler traits coming into my decision-making. In reality, most people are a mix, but will generally favor the traits of one more than the other. For both of these personality types, getting focused and productive presents the same challenges, however there is one factor that can be especially distracting – particularly for feelers – and that is emotion.

Not feeling in the "mood" or feeling upset or hurt at something or someone has the potential to completely derail your ability to *do that thing* you are saying that you are so desperate to achieve.

When you operate out of mood, you will never complete a project, and let's be real, regardless of whether you are a thinker or feeler, we are all subject to multiple moods and feelings each day.

- Feeling hungry?
- Itchy?
- Uncomfortable?
- Bored?
- Ticked off at your partner?
- Stressed at your kids leaving their dirty laundry around?
- Resentful at your co-worker receiving a promotion over you?
- Finding your task tedious and challenging?

If you allow these moods the chance, they will become excuses that prevent you from taking action.

"I'm not in the mood."

These five words can stop productive behavior dead in its tracks. Say it with a whiney child-like tone, (go on, I dare you!) and you will realize what you are really dealing with – your inner spoiled brat.

Every one of us has been a brat at some stage, but we generally have learned to control our inner brat as adults so that we can play nicely with others. Unfortunately, though, that control slips when we are trying to achieve tasks that require hard work and our bratty self that runs on feelings kicks in and we self-sabotage using all manner of our favourite procrastination techniques.

If you are a parent, you will be familiar with the scenario of your child behaving themselves immaculately for their teacher then throwing a tantrum as soon as they step foot in the house. We often subconsciously follow the same behavioral pattern. We focus hard for our bosses then throw an inner tantrum and can't be bothered when it is time to work hard for ourselves.

Yet if we don't learn to control our reactions to our moods, we will never achieve the thing that we are desperately wanting to achieve. We will be caught in that cycle of procrastination, despair and self-loathing and will find ourselves nowhere near rocking the on-purpose life that we had dreamed of.

ACTION TASKS:

- Try to catch yourself procrastinating or fluffing around when you should be focusing on a task that requires focus.
- Stop and ask yourself "what am I feeling?". If those feelings are negative, take the time to consider why you are feeling that way. Are they irrational or is there a valid reason for feeling that way? (Please note too that if you are feeling bleak, negative thoughts all the time for no rational reason, this is heading into a whole different realm – that of mental health. Your first step here should be to reach out to a trusted health professional for advice.)
- If there is something that you need to address, an unresolved argument for example, note it down. This way you are acknowledging that feeling and promising yourself that you will take the time later to deal with the situation.
- If it is hunger or thirst, sit back and determine whether these are true feelings or simply you procrastinating. If true feelings, set your timer for your designated work block and promise yourself that you will stop and enjoy a fabulous lunch once you have completed that session of focused work.
- If there is no obvious reason for why you are feeling "blah," change your physical state. Get out of your chair, do some star jumps and push-ups. Get that heart pumping and you will find that your mood brightens considerably.

- Determine that you are no longer going to give into your inner brat who doesn't *feel* like working. It's time that your brat was disciplined, so in the same way you wouldn't let your child stay home from school because they simply don't *feel* like going, tell your inner brat to be quiet and sit in the corner when they are screaming at you that they don't *feel* like working!

SECTION 6

ACCELERATION HACKS

"Start by doing what's necessary;
then do what's possible; and suddenly
you are doing the impossible."

~ FRANCIS OF ASSISI

HACK #18

Implement Systems

My precious friend Darlene, who lost her battle with cancer while I was writing this book, was the queen of systems. She turned her love of organization into a business called Systematic and brought peace and calm to so many people who were floundering in paperwork, facing overflowing wardrobes or, in my case, out of control pantries. In her quiet, graceful and non-judgmental way, she brought order to people's lives. It was from her example that I learned how *not* taking the time to create and implement systems is false economy.

Not creating systems means that you will find yourself going over and over the same activities, wasting time and creative energy that could have been applied to actually *doing* that thing you are wanting to achieve.

Be honest now, how many times have you played guess-the-password for various websites or wasted time retyping all of the same hashtags for a social media post? Systems and processes have the ability to free up so much of your time, allowing you to get on with the creative work that you should be doing. Yet we put off taking the time to create these systems as we are "too busy" chasing our tails instead.

Feeling too overwhelmed by what needs to be dealt with and don't know where to start?

My best advice – learned from the hard experience of trying to do everything myself – is to hire an organization expert or a Virtual Assistant, at least for a few hours, to help streamline your critical tasks. Even if you are a start-up on a shoestring budget, saving for a few hours of expert input will make a world of difference. At some point, you need to ask yourself if spending 15 hours importing contacts one by one into a new email server because you don't know how to import the entire data base is *really* the best use of your time … and yes, that was one of my own not-so-brilliant supposed cost-saving ventures! I ended up having to get a VA to do the job anyway in the end and could have saved myself so many hours that could have been better used focusing on the tasks that I *really* needed to do.

There are as many ways of streamlining as there are individuals but I have compiled a check list of ideas to prompt your thinking. Chances are you will read some like "make your bed" and wonder what on earth that has to do with systems and processes to help you achieve your goal. Trust me though, each suggestion listed has the ability to decrease the amount of clutter that you face every day, be it physical, mental or even in cyberspace. As we have already discussed, clutter contributes to sensory overload and overwhelm. Sorting and removing much of this clutter is one thing, but implementing systems to maintain and manage it going forward will help take away many of the distractions and noise that are hindering you from focusing on actually *doing* that thing you are meant to be doing which is living your life *on-purpose* and not in a reactionary state.

Personal Systems Tips

Put your clothes out the night before. If you're wanting to make a real difference, cut time and effort by keeping a minimalist selection of clothes. It's even worth investing into a stylist session to help you cull and plan your wardrobe.

If going to a gym or to any meetings, have those bags packed and ready the night before, making sure not to forget some of the basics: chargers, sunglasses and/or reading glasses, wallet, medications, mints, hair brush and personal items, as well as any planners or work due.

Have your car keys and a water bottle ready to be grabbed on your way out.

Keep a notebook on you at all times. Jot down any dates,

appointments and ideas then add them to your main planner every evening.

Review your planner every evening and keep a master list in it for all of the things that cross your mind that you need to do.

Develop the habit of cooking enough food at your evening meal so that you can pack your lunch with the leftovers ready for the next day.

Have a regular day scheduled in your diary once a fortnight or month depending on your needs where you drop off dry-cleaning and book your hair/dental/personal appointments.

Keep all incoming bills in the same location in your home and sort (and discard as necessary) mail as soon as it comes in the door. Likewise, flag all bills in your inbox as soon as they come in so that you can locate them all when you are ready to pay them.

Take ten minutes to clear the kitchen surfaces and living areas of an evening before bed.

Always make your bed of a morning.

Wipe down your bathroom surfaces with your used towel after showering and then throw it in the washing pile.

At least twice a year, thoroughly sort your pantry, medications, cleaning products and bathroom cabinet contents (I usually do these during spring and autumn).

Office Space Tips:

Tidy your desk whenever you have finished working. This applies for both the home and corporate environment.

Keep a drink bottle and coaster at your desk.

Keep mints at your desk.

Ensure that you have any stationery you need at hand.

If using in trays, allocate a regular time each day to sort, using the "one touch" method of actioning, delegating or disposing of the papers.

Online Mail Tips:

Every time a newsletter lands in your inbox that you don't want to or don't have the time to read, unsubscribe.

Create folders to move any tax-related invoices into immediately after payment.

Likewise, create folders for different categories of emails that do need to be saved for future reference e.g: domain information, passwords and links for online courses and products, testimonials.

Determine when you are going to check your email and stick to those times. Personally, I like to check in the morning, again around noon then again in the late afternoon.

Turn off your email notifications on your devices.

Take the time to automate a welcome series of emails for your business.

Social Media Tips:

Batch the creation of professional-looking Instagram posts using apps such as Canva and Wordswag.

Schedule social media posts ahead of time and consider using apps like Hootsuite, Publbox or Tailwind to schedule across multiple platforms.

Restrict checking social media sites to certain times of day. Again, I tend to do morning, noon and evening.

When you are checking social media at your allocated

times, instead of scrolling aimlessly, work your way systematically through your groups, replying to comments and private messages immediately.

If you are someone who is easily distracted by social media, establish the rule of not consuming before you create. In other words, do the work that requires the majority of your attention and focus before you scroll through other people's lives, views and opinions.

Business Tips:

If you are a business owner, you will probably be already aware that systems are the backbone to any successful business. You may want to consider having a specialist spend some time helping you implement these if you are in your start-up phase – it will be the gift that keeps on giving as you grow. Even if you are already in an established business and feeling lost, it's not too late to also invest in someone who can help you unravel the mess and establish systems. Some areas that you might want to consider systems for are:
- Health and safety
- Finances, including banking, wages and invoicing
- Insurances
- Product supply chain
- Stationery and office supplies
- Office rent, maintenance and utilities
- Advertising and marketing

- Client relationships
- Staff training and development

As you create and implement the systems that work for YOUR unique business, the key thing to remember is to *WRITE THEM DOWN!* Document your systems and create a manual for how your business works. This will prove invaluable for you in identifying where and why things have not worked, in on-boarding new staff and in the event of on-selling your business.

ACTION TASKS:
- Go through the checklists. Are there any areas that particularly jump out as being hotspots in your world that need to be systemized?
- Highlight these and brainstorm some ideas about how you could apply a system to them. Do this on paper so that you are actively engaged in the process.
- Choose three of these hotspots and determine to implement systems for them over the next week.
- At the end of that first week, review and tweak if need be then determine the next three hotspots to be tackled.
- Reach out to a specialist who can help you set up systems to support you going forward.

HACK #19
Create Your Dream Team

Setting out to achieve a dream can be a lonely journey, especially if your dream is something that you haven't ever attempted before. Chances are you won't be shouting from the rooftops that you are going to transform your body, write your first book, create your first art exhibition or build your first business until you've reached a stage in the process where you know that you WILL do it. (Unless of course, you are one of those social media come-with-me-for-the-ride type influencers – and prepared for the public pressure to succeed that comes along with that role!)

With any endeavour, there is that very real chance of failing. The more public the fail, the more embarrassing and debilitating the effect on you, meaning that getting back on the horse and trying again becomes that much harder. So many of us tend to keep our pursuit of our dreams and goals pretty close to our chests for this very reason, chipping out time to work on them privately and often falling prey to procrastination as we have no external accountability or deadlines to meet.

As an introvert who certainly doesn't like broadcasting all of my personal endeavours to the world, I totally get the desire to keep things close. The problem, however, is that the creative path is already often one of solitude and it is easy to lose perspective when you are too close to your creation. Our productivity suffers when we are stuck in our own heads, which is why it is so critical to create a dream team – your very own group of trusted people who can bring insight and wisdom to your life.

My own business mentors refer to their dream team as a Ring of Steel, and I have endeavoured to set up my own such circle of trusted individuals. The people in this group are not necessarily all close friends, but are people I respect, each with particular expertise who I can ask for advice and input. When I am stuck, need direction or simply need a kick up the butt, I know who I can turn to.

My dream team consists of my husband, my business mentors, my book coach, (I had procrastinated writing for so long that I knew that I needed to add this person to my team!) three close friends who are also in the speaking business and two trusted and patient VAs. Then there is the next layer of key people who I know I can turn to – my lawyer, my accountant, my GP of 20 years as well as some key friends here in NZ and abroad who I know I can reach out to any time.

If you are truly going to achieve that thing and *rock*

your life, the questions that you need to start asking yourself now are these:

> "Who are the people I want and need in my own dream team?"

> "Who are the people who I can trust, confide in, ask advice from and vent to when the going gets hard?"

> "Who will hold me accountable when I am fluffing around and not getting the work done to actually achieve my goal?"

For instance, let's say that your goal is to transform your body. Having worked in the fitness industry for years, I have seen many people with this desire, and in general, those who built a dream team around them were the ones that had the best success rate. As a personal trainer, I was privy to many of the hopes, dreams, health history and emotional ups and downs of those clients who included me as part of their dream team. My role was to encourage, instruct, motivate, sometimes cajole, and sometimes give the proverbial kick up the butt, as well as to measure their progress in relation to the time frame that we were working to.

A person with the goal of transforming their body may create a dream team that consists of:
- A nutritionist
- A personal trainer

- A mentor or friend who has completed their own transformation
- A supportive partner and/or close friend
- A GP or health professional
- A workout buddy

What is the goal that you are trying to achieve? Try to look at it objectively and reverse engineer it. What components need to be covered to bring it to fruition? What expertise would be necessary to support each of those components? Who do you know that has that expertise and do you trust them enough to bring them into your team?

Understand that your dream team is different to simply using professionals to fulfil certain tasks. I will be using a designer and a printer for this book at some stage, but they are not part of my dream team. Those roles are reserved for people who I trust, have a relationship with and who I know have my best interests at heart.

As well, these people have wisdom that comes from having the rungs on the board in their own particular fields of expertise.

Here are some suggestions for dream team members:
- Your partner
- Your closest friend
- Your closest medical professional
- Your trainer
- Your nutritionist
- Your lawyer
- Your financial advisor or accountant

- Your business mentor or coach
- Your art teacher
- Your writing coach
- Your music or theatre producer
- Your PA or VA
- Your agent or manager
- Your contemporary in another city or country

ACTION TASKS:

- Reverse engineer your goal and write a list of the expertise that you feel you need represented on your own dream team.
- Write a list of people who you know would fit each of those areas.
- Make contact with each person on your list and talk to them about their significance in your life. Buy them lunch, share the vision of the goal that you are wanting to achieve and listen to whatever wisdom they have to share.
- If there are people that you feel should be on your team but aren't, go through your networks, find the people who you think would fit and ask for introductions from mutual friends you trust and respect. It may take time, but these new people can be part of your outer layer while you build a relationship with them.

SECTION 7

ACTION HACKS

"There are risks and cost to action. But they are far less than the long-range risks of comfortable inaction."

~ JOHN F. KENNEDY

HACK #20

Intentional Action

Let's say that the thing that you are wanting to do is to write a book.

You follow your favorite authors on Amazon, stalk their websites and get onto their mailing lists.

You follow popular writing blogs and leave lots of well-thought out responses.

You follow more writers on Facebook and Instagram and engage in literary discussions.

You join author support groups online and encourage one another as you all identify your "why" for your books, your avatars that your books are aimed at and extol the merits of your preferred writing software.

You have a backlog of uncompleted "How to Write" courses.

You are an active participant in groups debating self-publishing over traditional publishing, along with every possibility in between.

You've spent hours cruising Fiverr and have a shortlist of preferred book designers and illustrators.

You are up to the play in regards to the best methods of marketing and promoting your book.

You are doing everything except WRITING the darn thing!

In short, you are taking plenty of action, but if your goal is to complete a book, none of the above action is intentionally moving you towards achieving this and, in complete transparency, I can say that I am speaking from experience.

Let's try another scenario. You might know the details of every gym within a 10 km radius of your home. You may understand every diet currently in vogue, have researched every exercise plan available, have the best gym wear, shoes and various bits of equipment floating around your house – yet have never actually committed to DOING the work needed to transform and strengthen your body.

See the pattern here?

It is so easy to fill every minute of time that we have with busy work that can seem related to the task that we are wanting to complete. If we aren't completely honest with ourselves, or open to having a member of our dream team point the obvious out to us, we can end up months or even years down the track, no closer to actually achieving our goal and living our life on-purpose, but frustrated and confused given all of the hours that we have spent supposedly working on that thing we have so earnestly said that we wanted to do.

Have you heard the expression "work ON your business, not IN your business?" This refers to the problem of business owners getting so caught up in the day-to-day activities of their business that could easily be delegated to others, that they lose perspective of the bigger picture and their business suffers as a result. All this while they are crying that they are too busy to scratch themselves.

The same principle holds true in achieving that thing that you want to achieve. If you get so caught up researching, reading and spending hours on simple tasks that could easily be outsourced, you will be actively sabotaging your progress. Time is such a precious commodity and you only have a limited amount of it to use towards bringing your goal to fruition. Being busy, but not in a way that is moving you towards achievement, is a deceptive habit to fall in to, and the quicker you can break it, the quicker you will start making progress.

Remember we talked about the false economy of trying to do everything ourselves, particularly when in a start-up phase? If your entire time is spent learning and working on various tasks that are not 100% in line with actually fulfilling your goal, you will never see your goal achieved. Sure, you might have an impressive website, fab social media, an active support group and even a perfectly immaculate house, but if your dream was to write a book, build a business, hold your own art exhibition or produce an album, NONE of these things will have contributed to the actual content you need. They are all periphery tasks that are best outsourced or, at the very least, worked on AFTER you have completed your main objective.

The saying that "any action is better than no action" doesn't really fly. While you could concede that it is marginally better than doing nothing at all, as we already discussed, action for the sake of action will keep you occupied, busy and feeling like you are on task, but will not bring you any closer to where you ultimately want to be. You will have wasted time, money and energy, all of which are usually in short supply at the start of a new project.

Better to rework that saying to "any *intentional action* is better than no action at all." Even if imperfect, intentional action that is specific, targeted and focused on the goal you are aiming for is going to have far more impact than had you not done anything at all. This way, even if, for instance, you are having a tough day with your writing where time has been scarce and your brain hasn't felt engaged – you have still managed to get some words and concepts out which can be edited and reworked, and therefore are still moving you towards your goal of writing that book.

ACTION STEPS:
- What is the actual, definitive task that you should be doing in order to achieve your goal? Writing? Painting? Creating your business plan? Composing? Writing your assignments? Memorizing that new language? Lifting those weights? Prepping that food? Practicing that instrument? If unsure, meet with one or more of your Dream Team members who have achieved the same goal and work it out with them.
- Write that task down on a large piece of paper headlined with this question: "Have you written/practiced/worked out/studied/painted today?" Make it bright, creative and eye-catching, then stick it on the side of your bathroom mirror or in your kitchen, or wherever you are guaranteed to see it every day.
- Commit to focused chunks of time where you will take your intentional action. Be conservative at first. It may just be one 25-minute session a day, however, during that time you will be ONLY working on that key task that you need to complete. You will be amazed at how far five straight days of working like this will propel you in comparison to the hours of distracted, unfocused busy work that you have been doing up to this point.
- Bargain with yourself and reward yourself when you succeed with completing your planned intentional behavior. Sample self-promises might be, "I will spend some time on social media after I have

studied for my exam for 2 x 40-minute blocks".
"I will enjoy some time off and go see a movie once I have completed a 45-minute focused session of high energy action each day this week."

HACK #21

Start Today!

It's time to take definitive action and START on that thing you are wanting to do! This might seem like a no-brainer, given that we have talked about your mindset, your physical environment, your health and wellbeing, your time management, your attitude, your ways of accelerating and taking action towards finally doing that thing that you have set as your goal, dream or desire. HOWEVER! I know that there will be some folks who read this book, along with every other mindset or time-management or productivity book out there, who are *still* yet to actually put pen to paper or paint to canvas etc.

If you fall into this category, or if you simply find yourself still dragging your feet in self-doubt after reading all of the previous 20 hacks, it's time to ask yourself some hard questions:

"Do I *really* want to achieve this goal?"

> "What would it *feel* like to achieve this goal?"
>
> "Do I *really* want to *rock* my life?"
>
> "What would it *feel and look* like to live my life *on-purpose*?"
>
> "If I were told that I only had days to live – would I be satisfied that I had *lived my life to the fullest?*"

What would it feel like if you didn't achieve your goal? If the pain of not achieving that goal feels enormous, you have your answer right there. It's time to harden up, soldier. Sit your butt down at your computer or at the gym, or wherever it needs to be, and take intentional, high energy, focused action *today*!

We talk to children about how not everything in life is fun. We teach them to eat vegetables instead of just ice-cream. We tell them to get outside and get some physical exercise instead of just playing on their X-box. We tell them that study and schoolwork are needed in order to prepare them for adult life and careers.

We expect children to learn discipline but then we make excuses for ourselves when it comes to applying our own focus and attention to something that requires hard work.

> "I'm too busy with other things."

"I'm not in the mood."

"I'm not feeling the muse."

"The planets didn't align."

The excuses are limitless and get more and more creative and elaborate when we are procrastinating on actually *doing* that thing and *rocking* our lives!!

One of the catchphrases that my personal training clients used to know me for and laugh at was "suck it up, princess" when they were balking at burpees or push-ups. My role as a personal trainer was to push these men and women further than they would have themselves and, without fail, there were always satisfied smiles when they achieved what they had previously thought was impossible.

It's now time to become your own personal trainer, holding yourself accountable and accepting no excuses when you are simply trying to dodge hard work.

It's time for you to suck it up, princess!

That side of you that wants instant gratification will always want to avoid hard or uncomfortable work. You'll suddenly find that you want to raid the fridge, scroll through Facebook or flick through the movie channel whenever it is time to focus. This is where you will need to discipline yourself to ignore that urge and simply start to take action right away.

I used to tell my gym clients that if they could push through those first 5–10 minutes of exercise, the endorphins would begin to kick in and the process would get easier. Perhaps not in the context of what had to be done, but certainly in the inner fight against it. I've found this same mind game effective for myself whether I am in the gym, practicing my instrument or sitting down to write. If I can push through all of the stories, the emotions, the sheer laziness and simply *start,* within 5–10 minutes, the resistance generally melts away and I find myself becoming engrossed with doing that thing that I actually really *want* to be working on.

Isn't it ironic that we procrastinate and resist doing that very thing that will move us towards achieving the dream that we have? For some people, that inner resistance can end up sabotaging their goal completely – but not you. This time is different isn't it?

How many people have said that they would love to write a book? A much larger number I can guarantee compared to those who actually start, and of these, the numbers are way higher than those who actually finish.

It's crunch time now.

Do you want to be the person who talks about the dream that they once had, or do you want to be the person who *achieves* that dream?

Do you want to live with the regret of never even having started the process needed to achieve your dream or do you want to experience the thrill of accomplishing that thing you are wanting to do? Do you want to live your life fully *on-purpose*, or just talk about it as a far off fairy-tale that may or may not actually happen?

What action are you going to take today to actually *start*?

ACTION TASKS:

- Identify what action you need to do in order to start working towards your goal. Is it to plan your book structure, visit that gym for a walk-through, book that art class, map out your assignment and study schedule or talk to your bank about getting that start up loan?
- Schedule your intended work times into your planner including one for TODAY!
- Let someone in your Dream Team know that you are starting your project today and also let them know that you are going to be sending them an accountability check in for the first five sessions that you complete.
- Put down this book and start TODAY!

A FINAL WORD FROM CAT

I believe in you.

Truly.

If you have made it this far through the book, this shows me that you are not someone who is wanting to settle for second best. No, you are someone who is honest and real about wanting to *rock* your life. You are someone who is brave enough and audacious enough to believe that you exist for a purpose that is larger than yourself. You've reached the point where you don't want to simply go through the motions of existing anymore – you want to live your life *on-purpose*.

There is no special magic that causes some people to work towards their goals with laser focus while others with similar goals can't seem to get started. In the same way, none of the hacks I have listed here are rocket science – however I can guarantee that the former group of people who are actually *doing* the thing that they set out to do have implemented many of them during their journey.

If you commit to reading these 21 Hacks and implementing the action steps I have given you, I can guarantee that your life will not be the same in a month's time. You will feel energised, positive, productive, resilient, in control, focused, full of self-belief and not hoping to rock your life – but actually *doing* it!

You see, there is a secret I have been holding all through this book until this last section. Living a life on-purpose is not something that you "arrive at". It is something that you actively do every day as you journey through life. If you know that you have a purpose to fulfil – be it charitable, creative or professional – and you live your life in such a way that you are intentionally taking action every day towards fulfilling that mission – then you are truly *rocking* your life and living it *on-purpose*.

People who live their lives like this are the people who change the world – because they impact and change their communities as they do that thing that they are uniquely called to do.

Isn't it time that you joined them?

Isn't it time that you *rocked* your life?

Isn't it time that you chose to live your life *on-purpose*?

You've got the tool box of hacks to help you get going, so start today! It's really as simple as that.

Again – I believe in you, and I would love to hear how implementing these 21 Hacks have helped you rock *your* life, and impacted those around you!

Cat x
Auckland, 2019

ACKNOWLEDGEMENTS

I am blessed to have had so many great people who helped with this book and the first call out goes to the man who has always had my back, believed in me and challenged me to stop playing small over the years – my husband of over 30 years, Leli. Lots of love and thanks also goes out to the rest of my family who have always supported me and my cat addiction – my children, Bronte, Jonathan and my lovely daughter in law Natalie. As well, my parents Don and Jan Byrne who unknowingly modelled so many of these hacks as I grew up.

I really found my tribe when I joined the Professional Speakers Association of New Zealand and the encouragement, support and relationships that I have built there have directly shaped my own message and mission. From connecting with my wonderful international business mentors Mike Handcock and Landi Jac, to the on the ground support and invaluable input I have received from the New Zealand Certified Speaking Professionals as the result of winning the 2019 National Fast-Track Scholarship – I am so incredibly grateful. Special thanks also go to the current President Darren Pratley and close friends and colleagues Cat Levine, Kirsty Salisbury, Lisa Dudson, Eloise Tzimas and Diana Thompson for their advice, support, encouragement and a heck of a lot of laughs. I love that we are all choosing to *rock* our lives and make an impact in our communities.

Special shout outs too to some of the other incredible women in my life who have shared a wine, their wisdom and a laugh with me and live their lives unapologetically on-purpose: Kiri-Maree Moore, Angela Raspass, Catherine Grace O'Connell, Pauline Stockhausen, Kat Soper, Shannon Conaglen, Amanda Betts, Debra Chantry, Christine Walter, Ann van Engelen, Vicki Jeffels and Natalie Cutler-Welsh. In your own unique ways, you ladies all inspire me.

Huge love too to my online tribe of local and international friends who are ROCKING their midlife, their wellness and their businesses in my online communities: you guys are amazing!

There is truly something powerful about women inspiring and empowering other women!

On to the book. To my beta-readers who slogged through the early draft – Ellen Bialostocki, Karen Barnett and Simon Diprose and the team at Indie Experts – thank you so much. I truly appreciate your time, patience and input. Finally, to the lady who has acted as my own personal trainer for book production – alternatively encouraging, cajoling and kicking my butt to meet deadlines – Dixie Maria Carlton of Indie Experts. I am so glad that we connected and are on this journey together! *Cheers girlfriend and here's to the next 21 Hacks!*

ABOUT CAT COLUCCIO

Cat Coluccio is an Author, a Reinvention Coach, the host of the **Rocking Midlife® Podcast** and **Community** – *and a champion of midlife women.*

A qualified Educator, Personal Trainer and Life Coach, Cat is passionate about seeing women empowered to stop procrastinating, identify their values and goals, take intentional action and build purposeful lives and businesses, creating a legacy for their families and communities.

At home speaking on both live or virtual stages, Cat has been a featured guest on numerous international podcasts and summits, as well as in national print publications, television and radio shows.

A transplanted Australian, Cat resides in New Zealand with her husband, children and grandson, along with far too many cats, chooks and sheep. She's partial to a glass of prosecco and a laugh with friends, good chocolate, great books, and lives by her personal philosophy: *"It's never too late to have a new beginning in life."*

WANT MORE CAT?

Check out Cat's other 21 Hacks books!

21 Hacks to ROCK your Life – the TEEN Edition!
*Stop Stuffing Around, Get Focused
and Create a Life that ROCKS!!*

21 Hacks to ROCK your Midlife!
Release the Past, Dare to Dream and Create your Legacy!

Find these titles and more by following
Cat's author page HERE: https://amzn.to/3A2XoKu

Want more FREE resources to help you ROCK your life?

Check out Cat's website HERE: www.catoluccio.com

Let's get Social!

F: @catcoluccio
IG: @catcoluccio
Pin: @catcoluccio
YT: @catcoluccio

Want some cool clothing, gifts and motivating printables?

Check out Cat's 2 ETSY shops HERE:

Rocking Midlife®:
https://www.etsy.com/nz/shop/rockingmidlife

Rock your Side-Hustle:
https://www.etsy.com/nz/shop/RockyourSideHustle

ENDNOTES

1 Sheard, M., & Golby, J. (2006). Effect of a Psychological Skills Training Programme on Swimming Performance and Positive Psychological Development. International Journal of Sport and Exercise Psychology, 4, 149–169.
2 Peters, Madelon M L et al. "Manipulating optimism: Can imagining a best possible self be used to increase positive future expectancies?" (2010).
3 Loh, KepKee et al. "Higher Media Multi-Tasking Activity Is Associated with Smaller Gray-Matter Density in the Anterior Cingulate Cortex." *PloS one* (2014).
4 https://www.umassmed.edu/cfm/about-us/people/2-meet-our-faculty/kabat-zinn-profile/
5 Costa, Arthur L. and Bena Kallick. "Learning and Leading with Habits of Mind: 16 Essential Characteristics for Success." (2009).
6 Ajala, Emmanuel Majekodunmi. "THE INFLUENCE OF WORKPLACE ENVIRONMENT ON WORKERS' WELFARE, PERFORMANCE AND PRODUCTIVITY." (2012).
7 T Bernstein, Ethan and Stephen Turban. "The impact of the 'open' workspace on human collaboration." *Philosophical transactions of the Royal Society of London. Series B, Biological sciences* (2018).

8 Banbury, Simon P. and Dianne C. Berry. "Disruption of office-related tasks by speech and office noise." (1998).
9 Clark, Charlotte et al. "Exposure-effect relations between aircraft and road traffic noise exposure at school and reading comprehension: the RANCH project." *American journal of epidemiology* 163 1 (2006): 27–37.
10 CEO The Sound Agency https://resonics.co.uk/12-ways-noise-affects-employee-wellbeing-health-productivity/
11 Padmanabhan, Rajiv et al. "A prospective, randomised, controlled study examining binaural beat audio and pre-operative anxiety in patients undergoing general anaesthesia for day case surgery." *Anaesthesia* 60 9 (2005): 874–7.
12 https://thriveglobal.com/stories/these-7-tips-will-help-you-sleep-better-backed-by-science/
13 Chellappa, Sarah L. et al. "Acute exposure to evening blue-enriched light impacts on human sleep." *Journal of sleep research* 22 5 (2013): 573–80.
14 Obradovich, Nick et al. "Nighttime temperature and human sleep loss in a changing climate." *Science Advances* (2017).
15 https://www.health.harvard.edu/staying-healthy/5-of-the-best-exercises-you-can-ever-do
16 Panza, Francesco et al. "Contribution of Mediterranean Diet in the Prevention of Alzheimer's Disease." (2018).
17 "Nutrient Reference Values for Australia and New Zealand" www.moh.govt.nz
18 Willis, Lauren M. et al. "Modulation of cognition and behavior in aged animals: role for antioxidant- and essential fatty acid-rich plant foods." *The American journal of clinical nutrition* 89 5 (2009): 1602S–1606S.
19 Masento, Natalie et al. "Effects of hydration status on cognitive performance and mood." *The British journal of nutrition* 111 10 (2014): 1841–52.
20 Claessens, Bjc Brigitte et al. "A review of the time management literature." (2007).

21 Cirillo, Francesco. "The Pomodoro Technique: The Life-Changing Time-Management System." (2018).
22 Klassen, Robert M. et al. "Academic procrastination of undergraduates: Low self-efficacy to self-regulate predicts higher levels of procrastination." (2008).
23 Ibid.
24 Malik, Maria Ashraf. "The Relationship between Myers Briggs Type Indicator (MBTI) and Emotional Intelligence among University Students." (2014).

REFERENCES

Ajala, Emmanuel Majekodunmi. "The Influence of Workplace Environment on Workers' Welfare, Performance and Productivity." (2012).

Banbury, Simon P. and Dianne C. Berry. "Disruption of office-related tasks by speech and office noise." (1998).

Chellappa, Sarah L. et al. "Acute exposure to evening blue-enriched light impacts on human sleep." *Journal of sleep research* 22 5 (2013): 573–80.

Cirillo, Francesco. "The Pomodoro Technique: The Life-Changing Time-Management System." (2018)

Claessens, Bjc Brigitte et al. "A review of the time management literature." (2007).

Clark, Charlotte et al. "Exposure-effect relations between aircraft and road traffic noise exposure at school and reading comprehension: the RANCH project." *American journal of epidemiology* 163 1 (2006): 27–37.

Costa, Arthur L. and Bena Kallick. "Learning and Leading with Habits of Mind: 16 Essential Characteristics for Success." (2009).

Harvard Health: https://www.health.harvard.edu/staying-healthy/5-of-the-best-exercises-you-can-ever-do

Jon Kabat-Zinn: https://www.umassmed.edu/cfm/about-us/people/2-meet-our-faculty/kabat-zinn-profile/

Klassen, Robert M. et al. "Academic procrastination of undergraduates: Low self-efficacy to self-regulate predicts higher levels of procrastination." (2008).

Loh, KepKee et al. "Higher Media Multi-Tasking Activity Is Associated with Smaller Gray-Matter Density in the Anterior Cingulate Cortex." *PloS one* (2014).

Malik, Maria Ashraf. "The Relationship between Myers Briggs Type Indicator (MBTI) and Emotional Intelligence among University Students." (2014).

Masento, Natalie et al. "Effects of hydration status on cognitive performance and mood." *The British journal of nutrition* 111 10 (2014): 1841–52.

Ministry of Health NZ: www.moh.govt.nz

Obradovich, Nick et al. "Nighttime temperature and human sleep loss in a changing climate." *Science Advances* (2017).

Padmanabhan, Rajiv et al. "A prospective, randomised, controlled study examining binaural beat audio and pre-operative anxiety in patients undergoing general anaesthesia for day case surgery." *Anaesthesia* 60 9 (2005): 874–7.

Panza, Francesco et al. "Contribution of Mediterranean Diet in the Prevention of Alzheimer's Disease." (2018).

Peters, Madelon M L et al. "Manipulating optimism: Can imagining a best possible self be used to increase positive future expectancies?" (2010).

Resonics: CEO The Sound Agency https://resonics.co.uk/12-ways-noise-affects-employee-wellbeing-health-productivity/

Sheard, M., & Golby, J. (2006). Effect of a Psychological Skills Training Programme on Swimming Performance and Positive Psychological Development. International Journal of Sport and Exercise Psychology, 4, 149–169.

T Bernstein, Ethan and Stephen Turban. "The impact of the 'open' workspace on human collaboration." *Philosophical transactions of the Royal Society of London. Series B, Biological sciences* (2018).

Thrive Global: https://thriveglobal.com/stories/these-7-tips-will-help-you-sleep-better-backed-by-science/

Willis, Lauren M. et al. "Modulation of cognition and behavior in aged animals: role for antioxidant- and essential fatty acid-rich plant foods." *The American journal of clinical nutrition* 89 5 (2009): 1602S-1606S.

www.ingramcontent.com/pod-product-compliance
Lightning Source LLC
Chambersburg PA
CBHW071928290426
44110CB00013B/1525